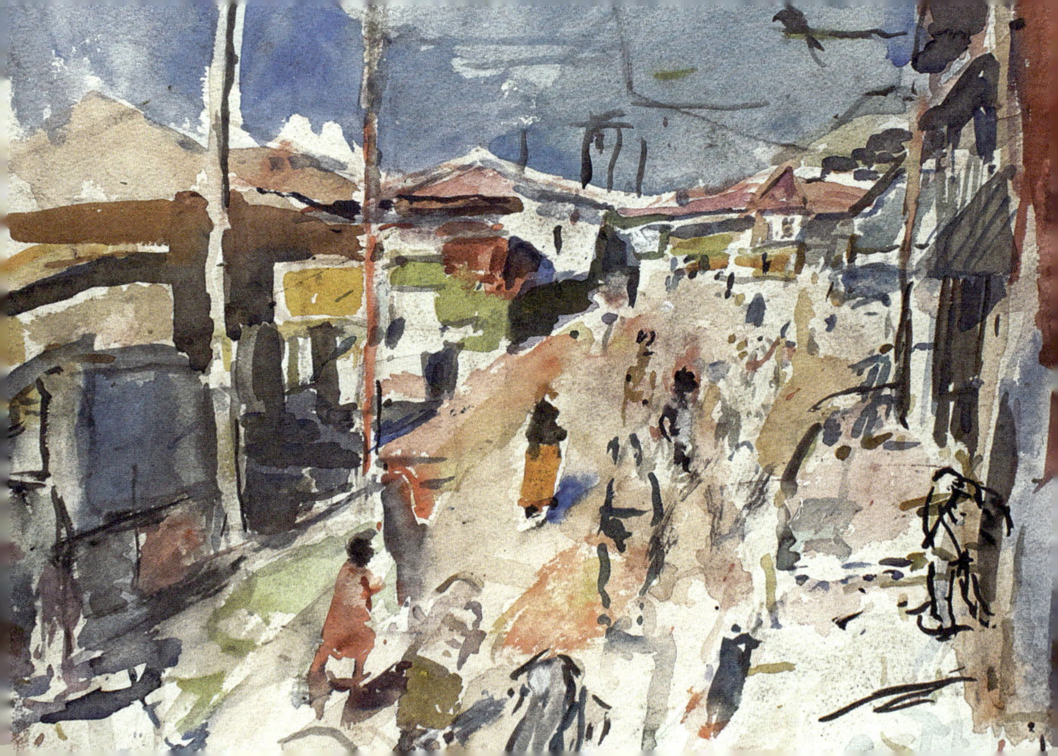

Anthony Eyton

AN INDIAN SKETCHBOOK

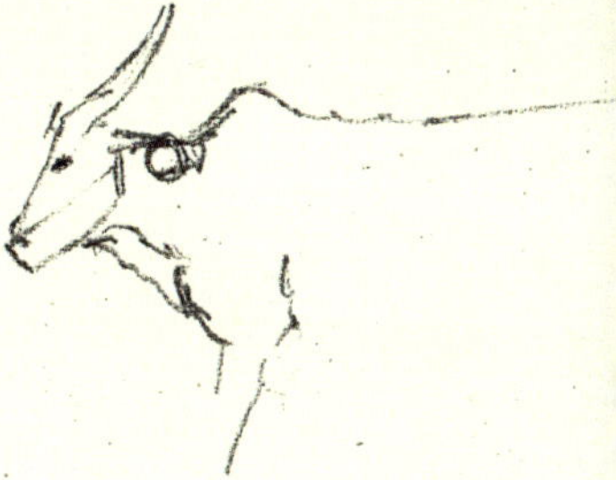

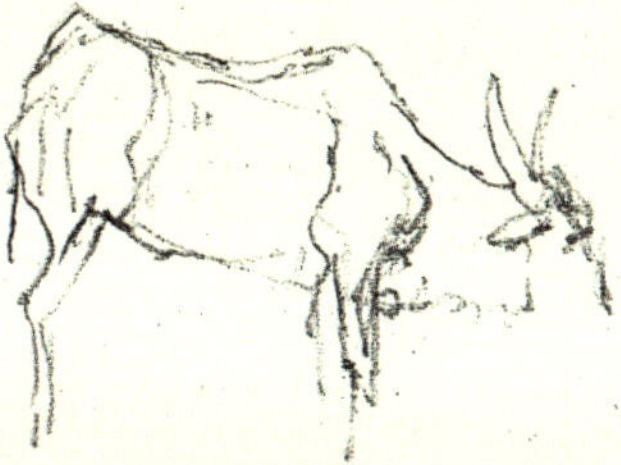

Royal Academy of Arts

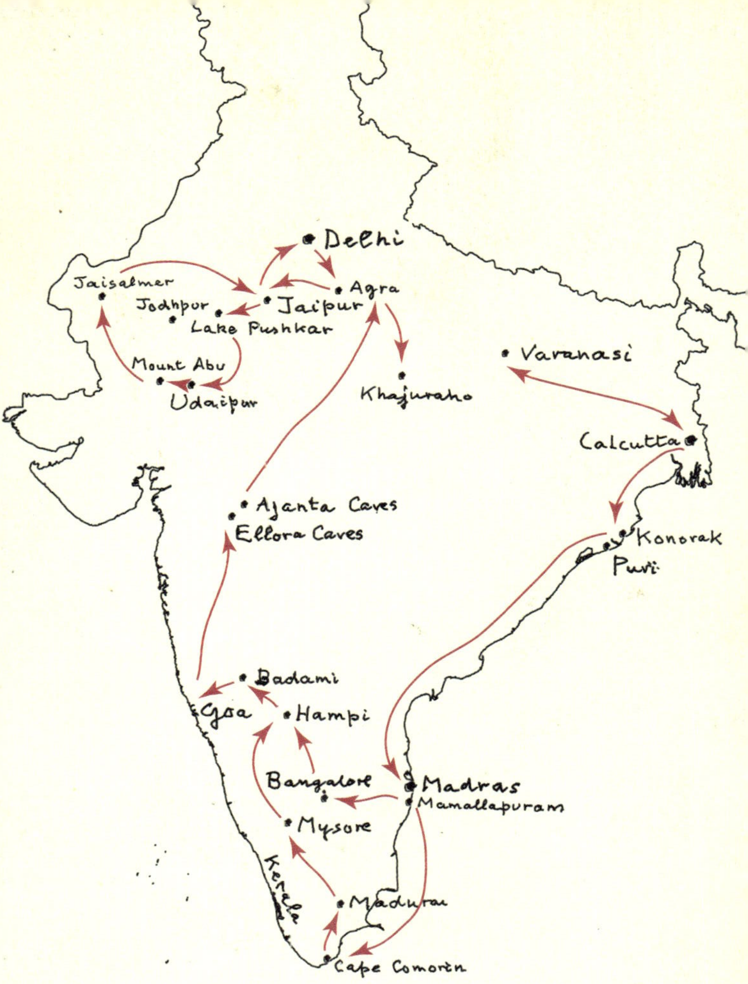
Delhi
Jaisalmer
Agra
Jodhpur
Jaipur
Lake Pushkar
Varanasi
Mount Abu
Udaipur
Khajuraho
Calcutta
Ajanta Caves
Ellora Caves
Konorak
Puri
Badami
Goa
Hampi
Bangalore
Madras
Mamallapuram
Mysore
Kerala
Madurai
Cape Comorin

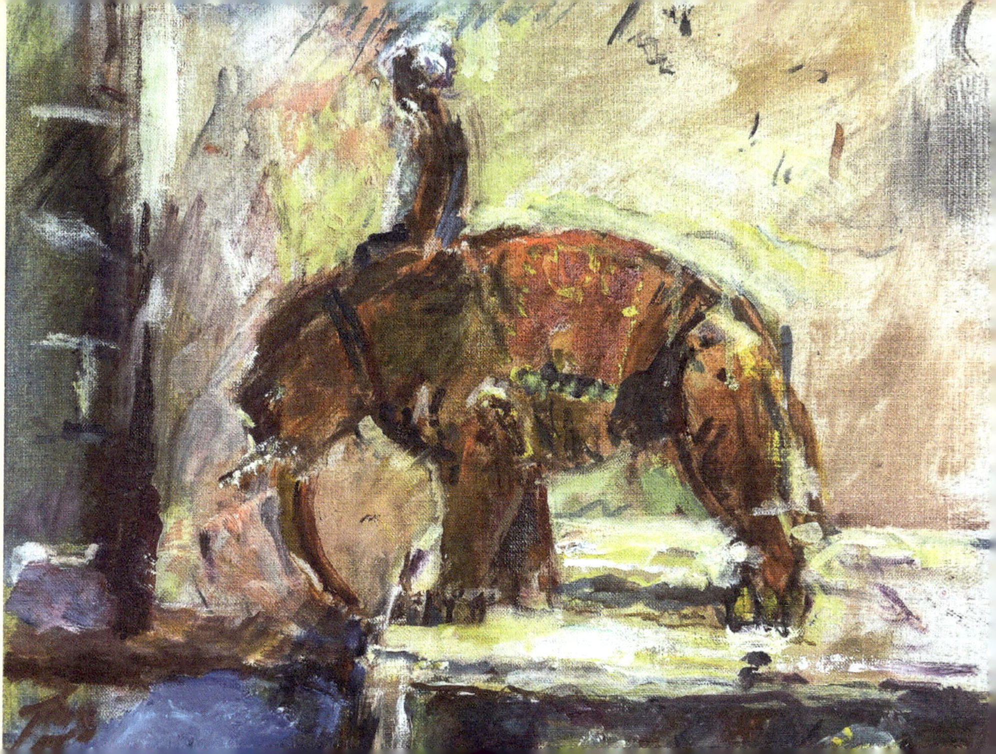

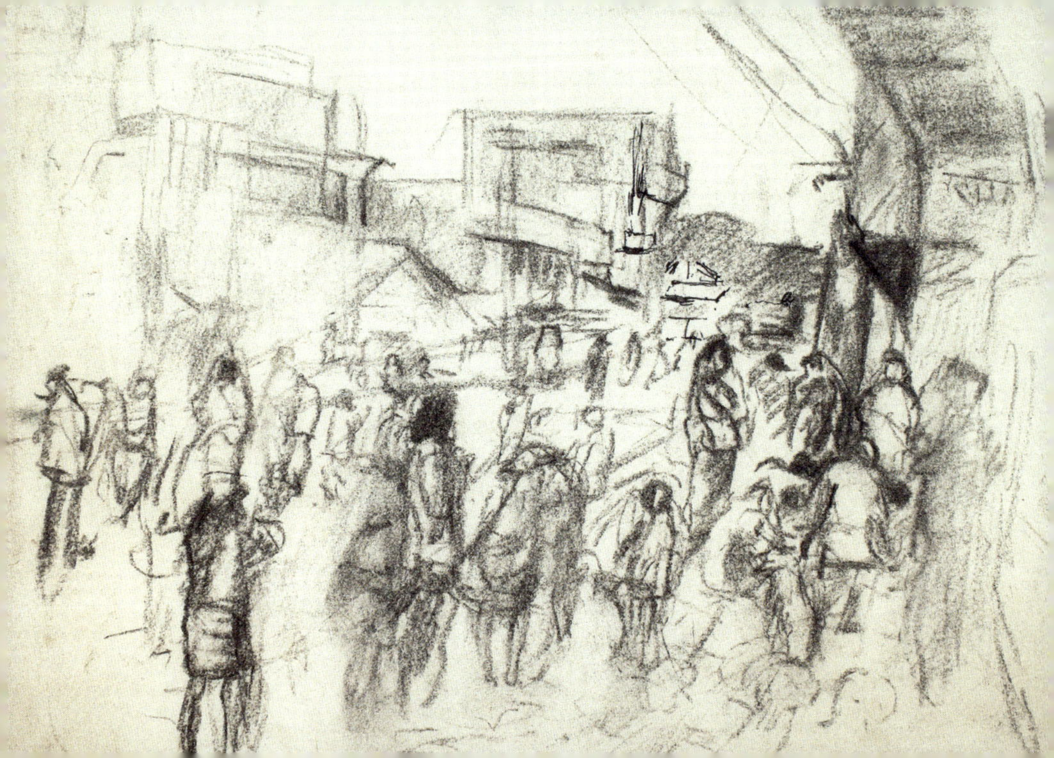

I made my first visit to India in November 1978. I was there for five months, and I still recall the sadness of leaving my family for such a long time.

Arriving in Delhi was a great culture shock, the noise and seething crowds. There was a lot to cover. I travelled by bus and train: temples, other sites, the many wonderful people who live there, and my fellow travellers. I made lots of drawings, chiefly pastels and watercolours. I was devastated when my sketchbook, drawings and camera were stolen from me on a train in Calcutta. They were irreplaceable!

While in Calcutta I spent time with the film director Satyajit Ray and the composer Ravi Shankar. We showed each other our drawings. I visited so many other places: Khajuraho, Mamallapuram, Chengalpattu, Delhi, Mysore, Cape Comorin, Hampi, the Ajanta Caves at Aurangabad, Madurai.

It's important to be careful about drinking water and one's diet in India, but I slipped up and had bad dysentery for a fortnight in Varanasi, which ultimately led me to the Hospital for Tropical Diseases in London with liver damage.

I revisited India five times after that initial trip: Udaipur, Goa, Jaisalmer, Jaipur, Puri, Kerala, the Ellora Caves at Aurangabad, Bangalore, the caves and monuments at Badami, and Lake Pushkar for the three-day camel fair.

Many of the drawings I made in 1978 and on my subsequent trips are included here. When drawing in India I saw Poussin constantly, in colour and structure; he integrates man and nature. A lot of people talked to me as I worked. Indian children are so curious, and sometimes pester. Things certainly turned out differently from the way I'd expected. And somehow in India there's always activity, and sunshine. So much is happening!

Anthony Eyton RA

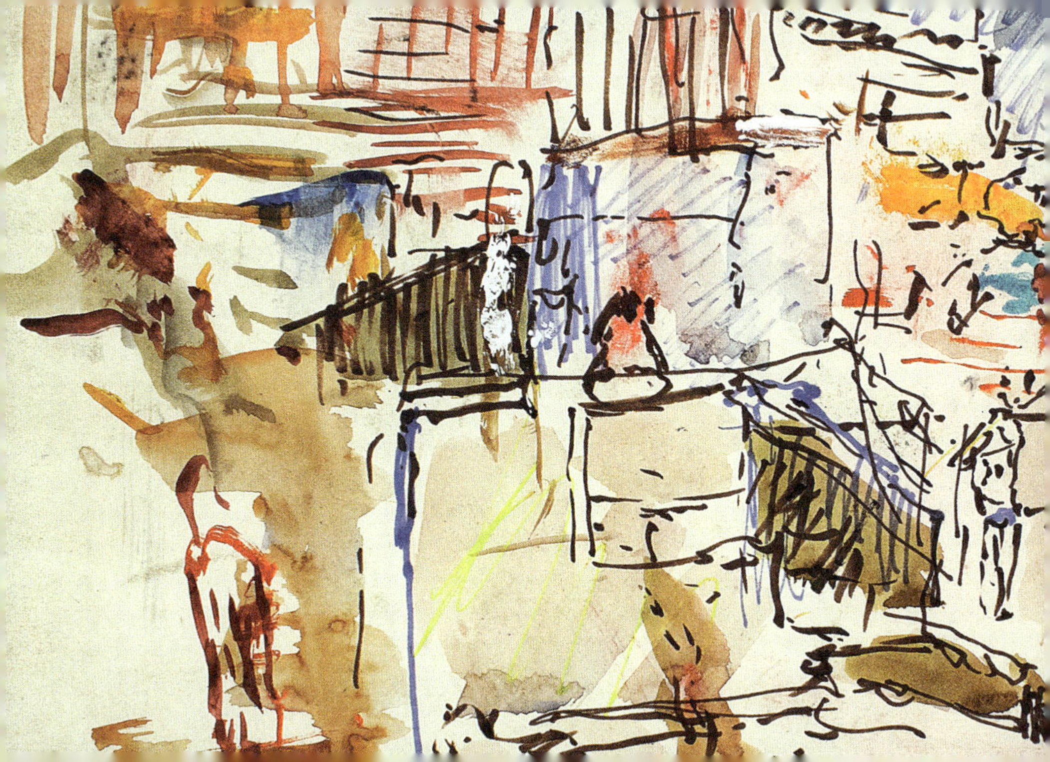

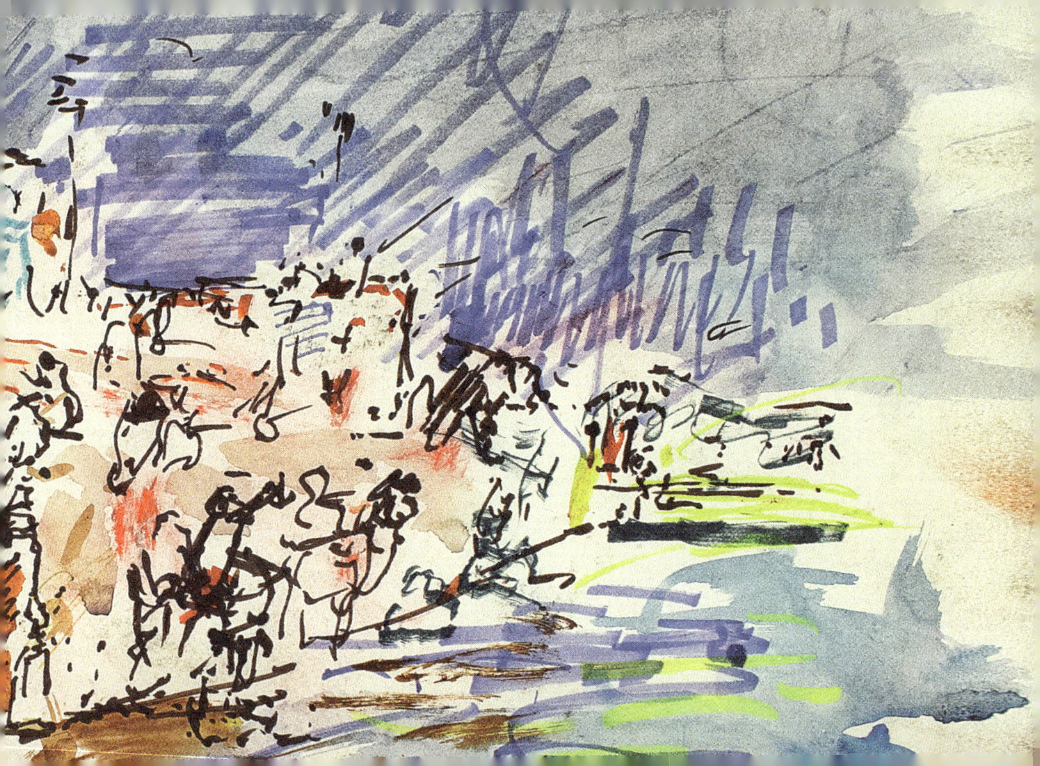

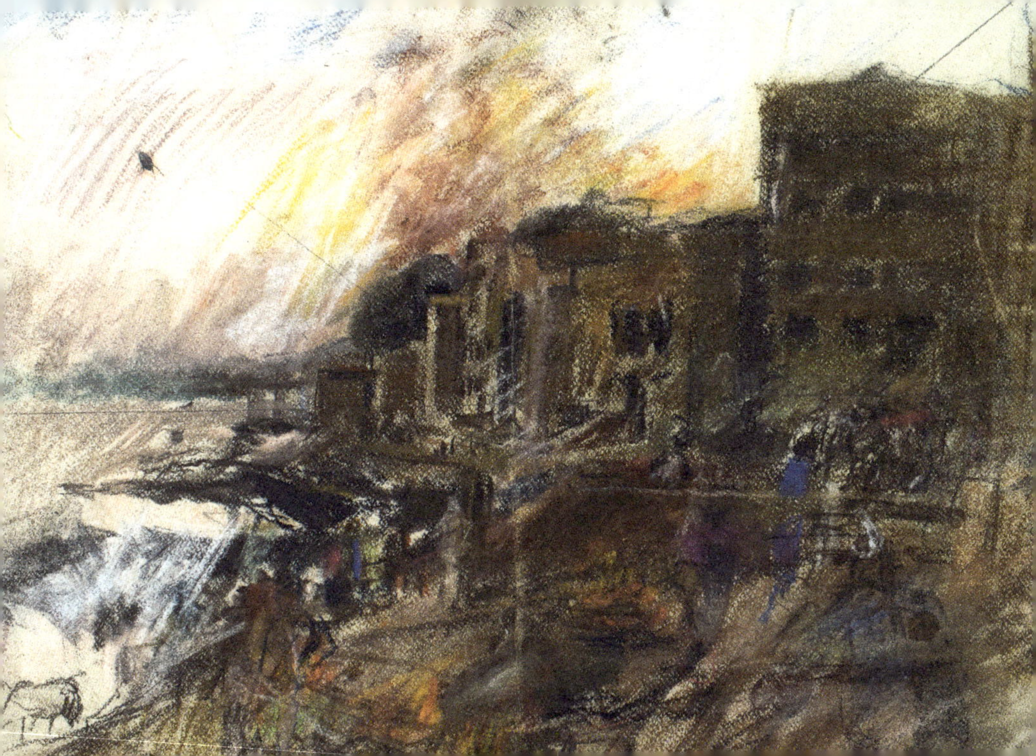

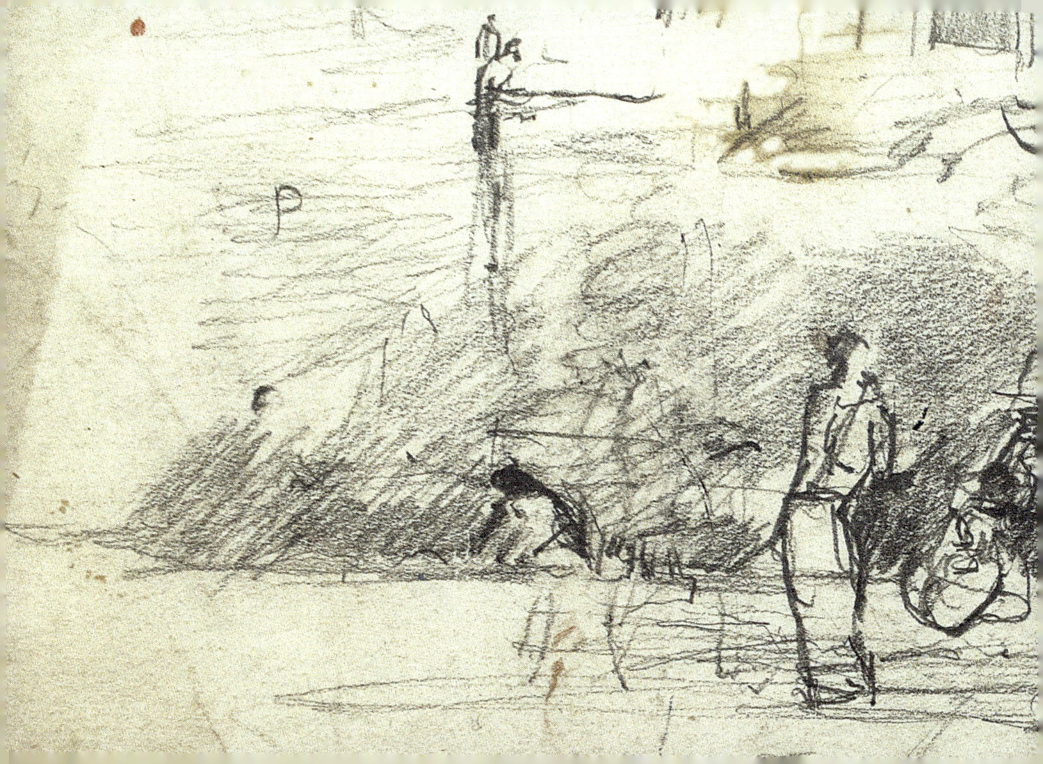

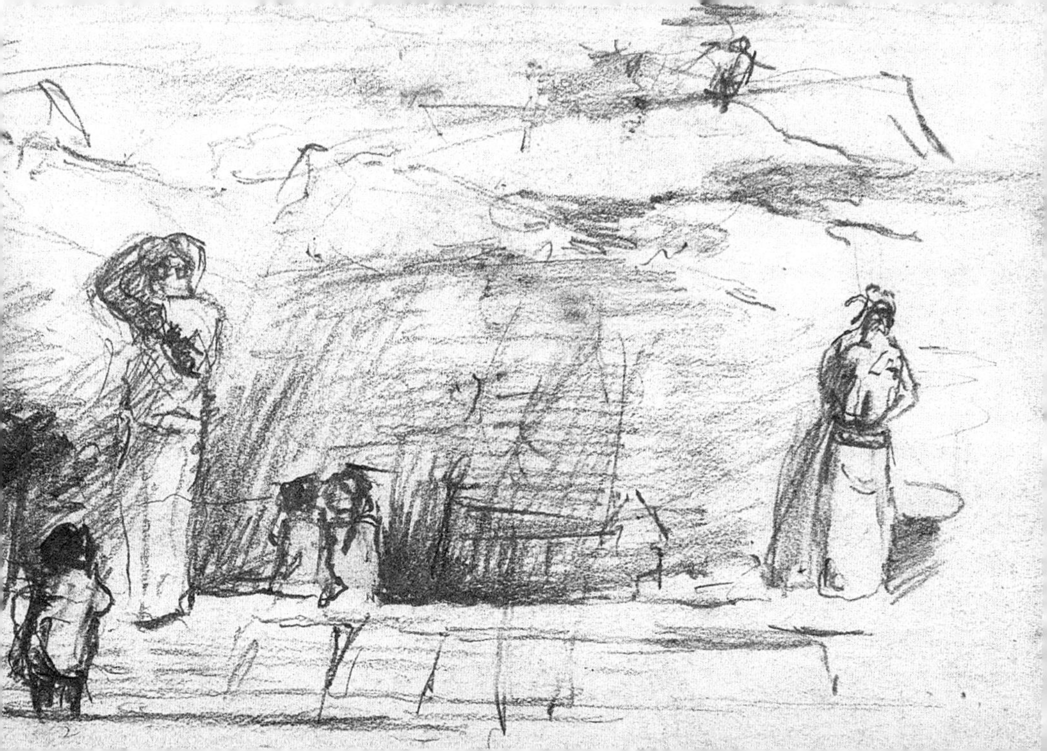

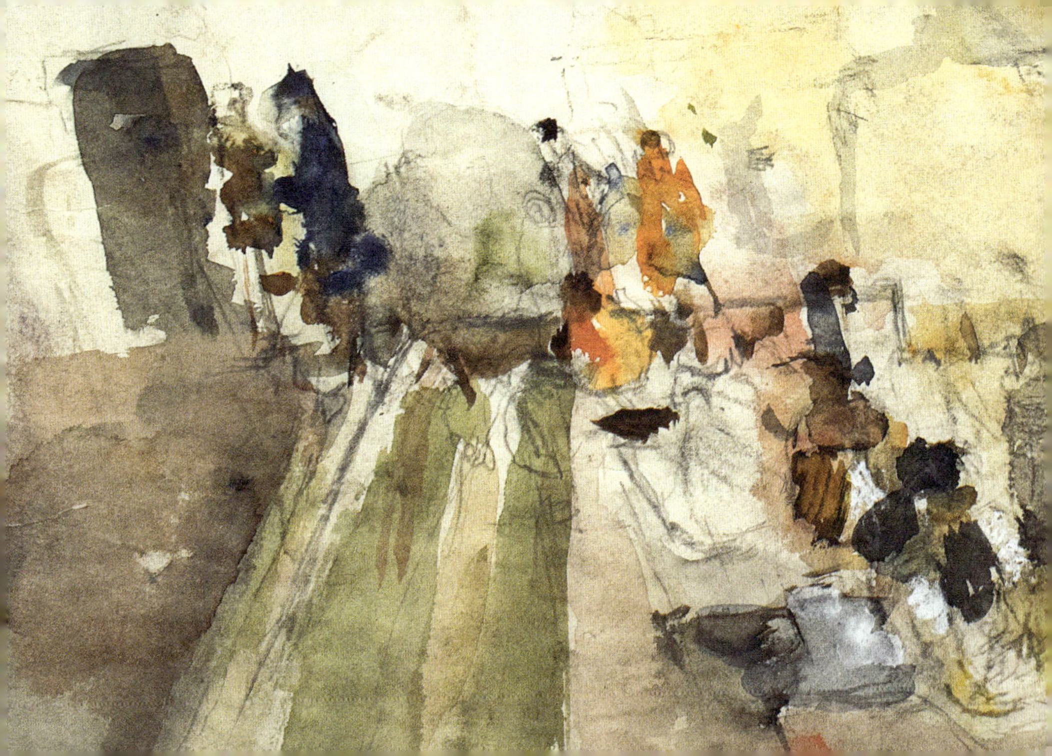

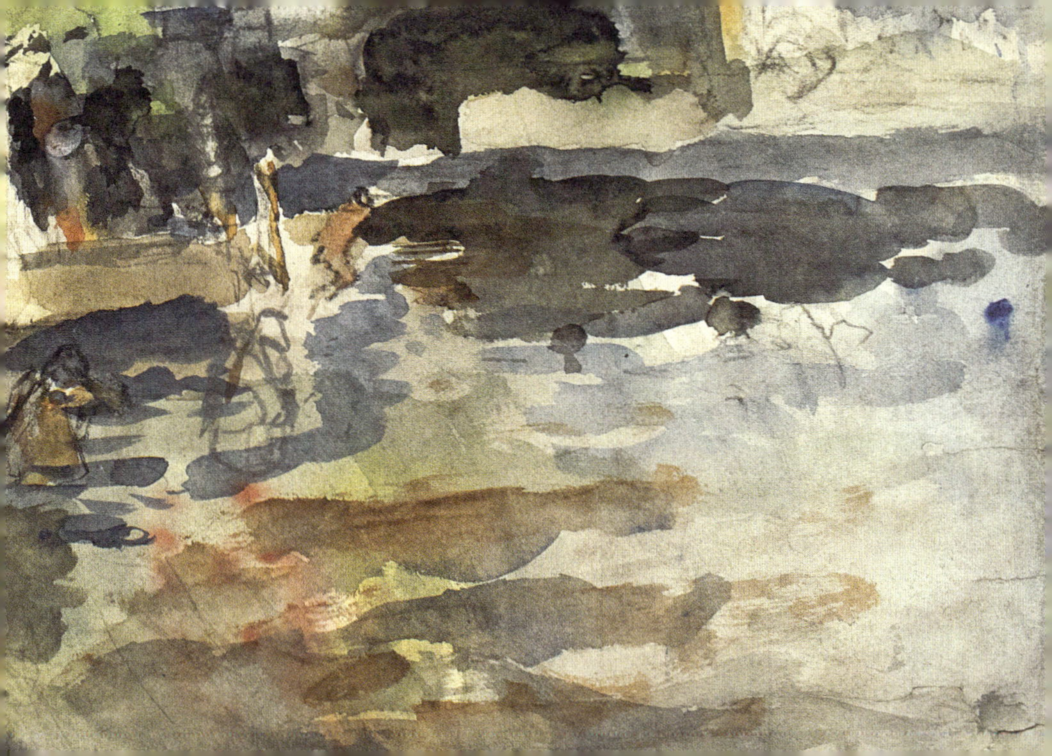

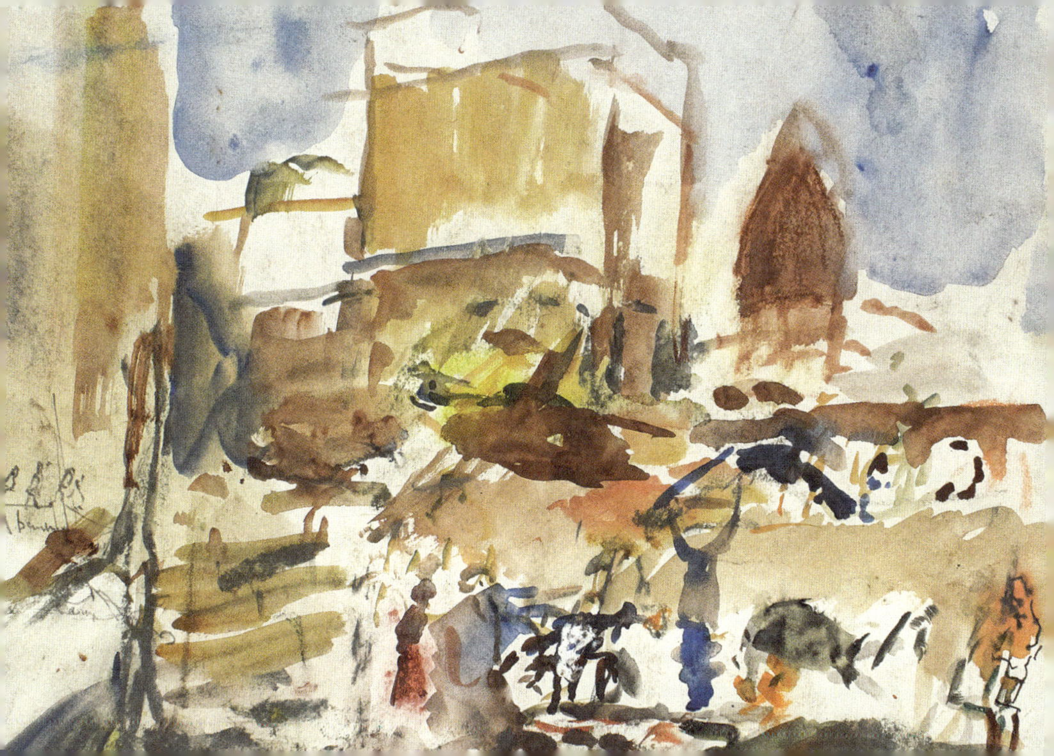

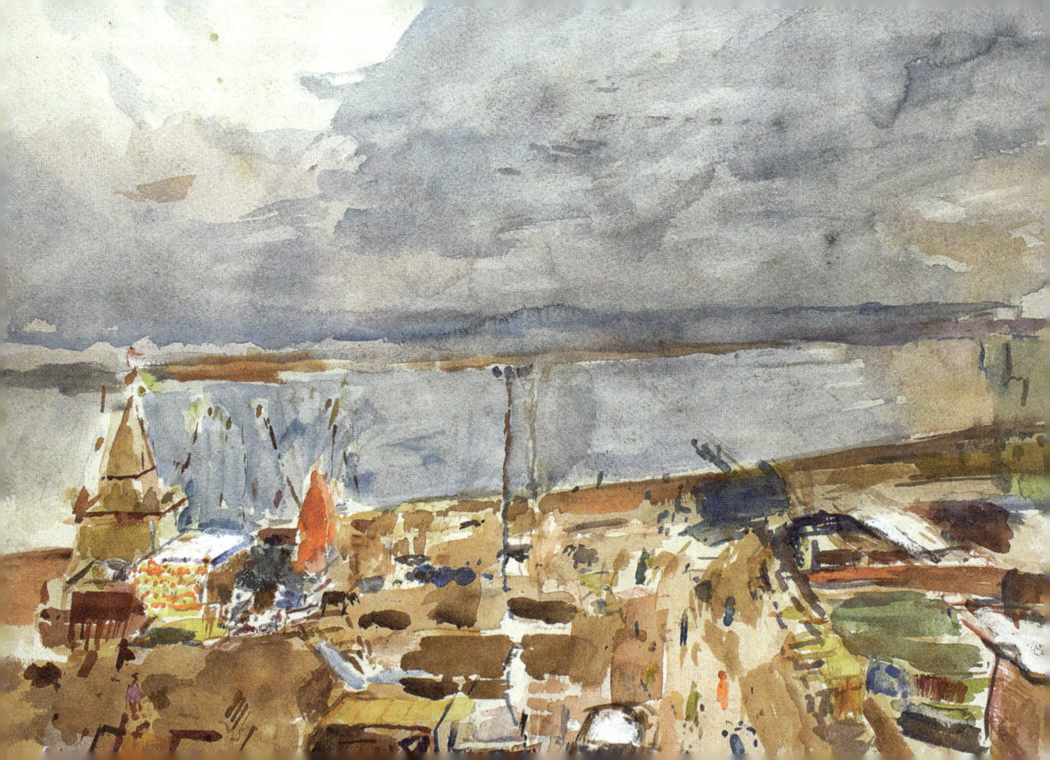

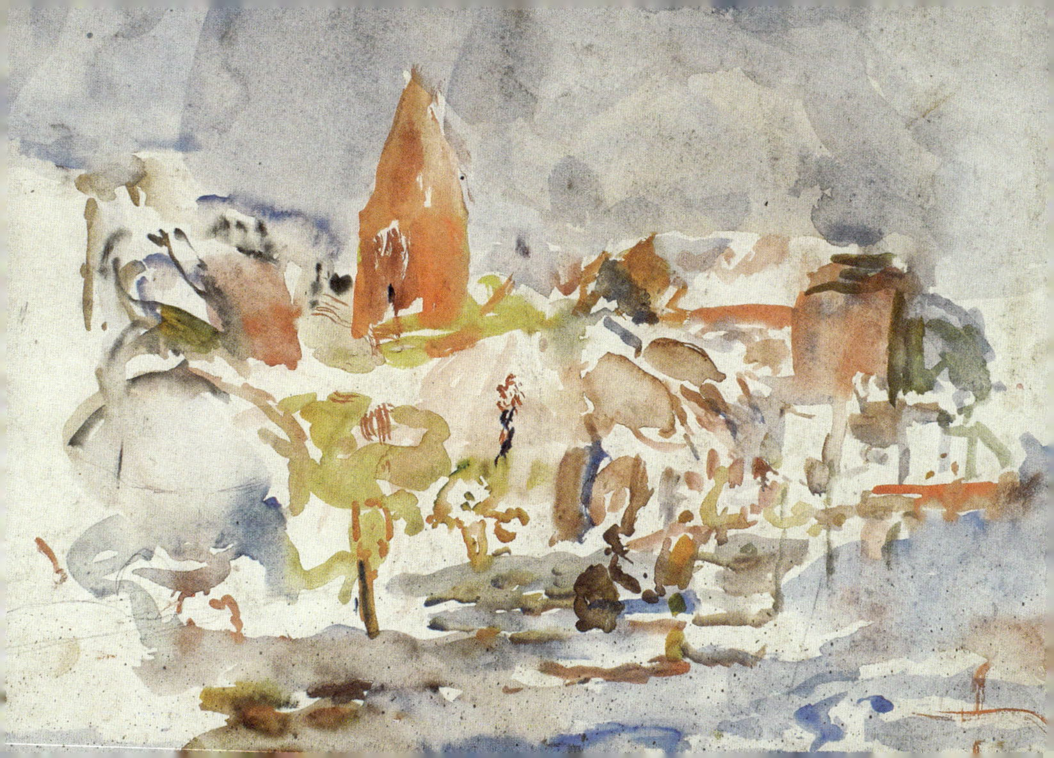

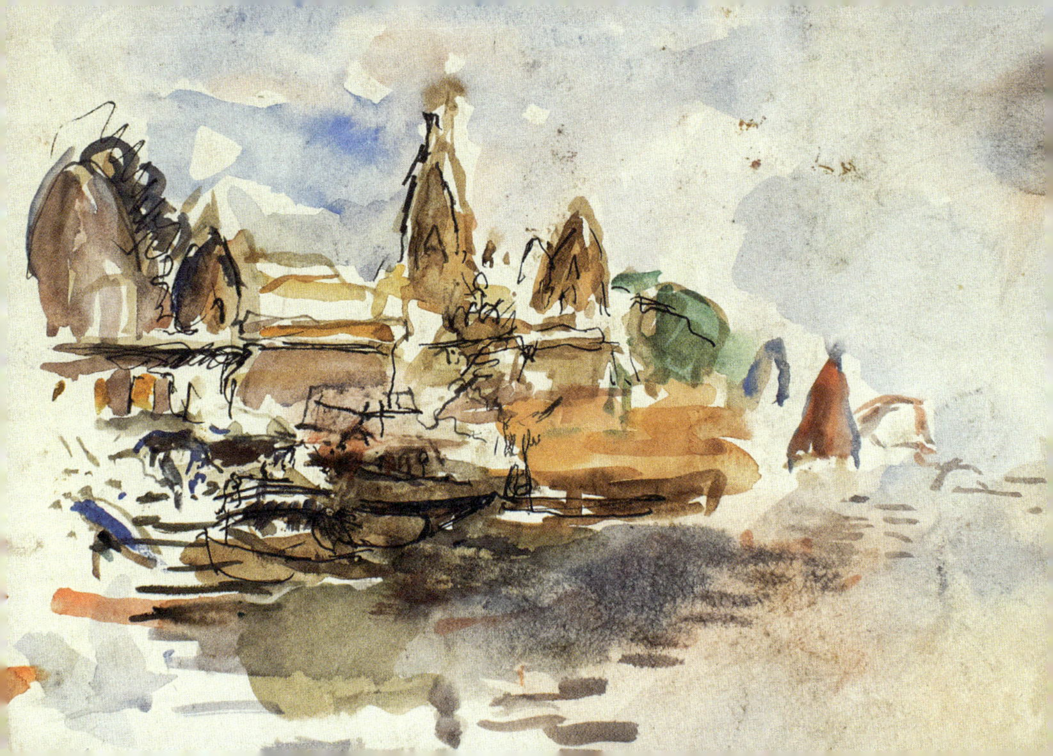

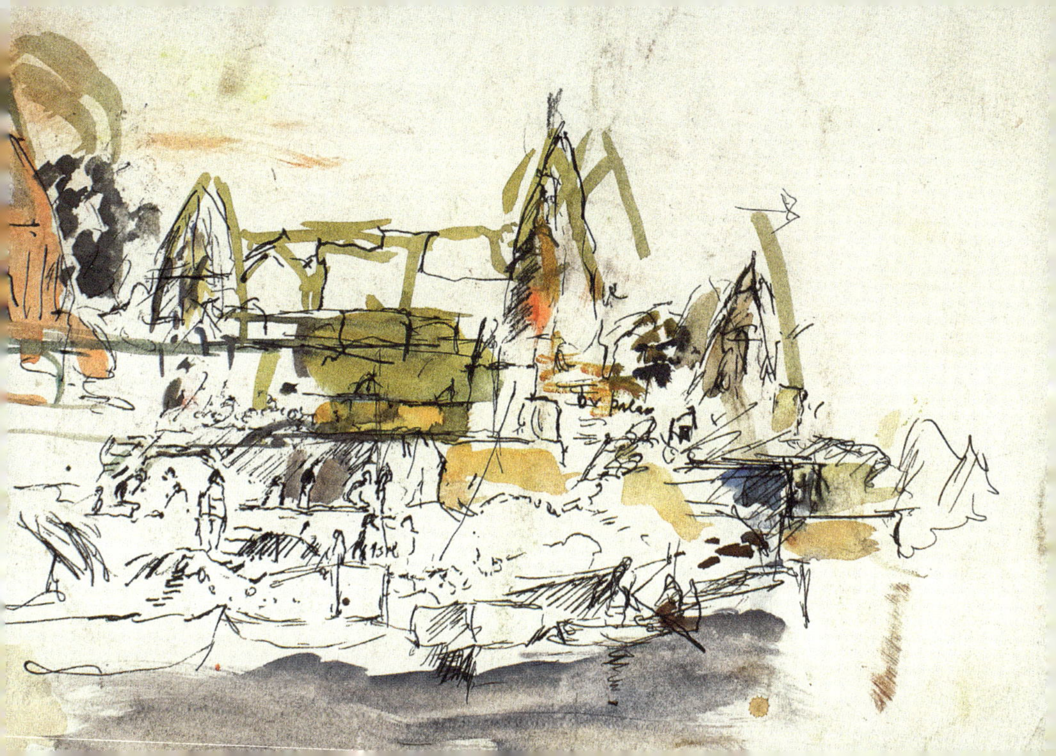

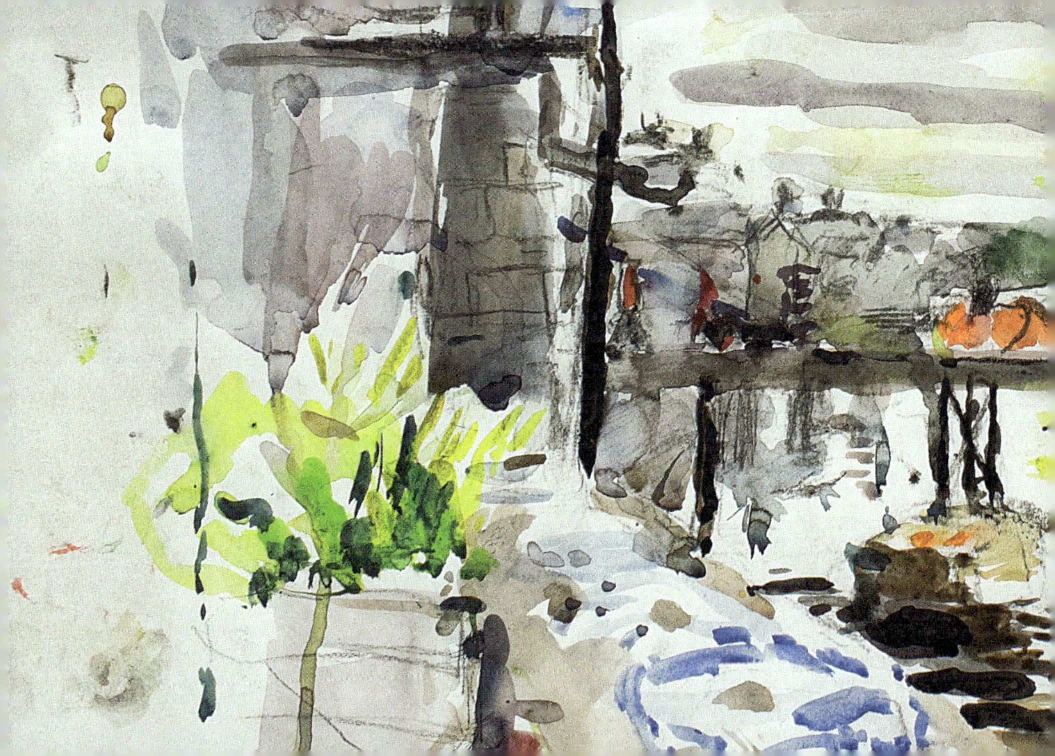

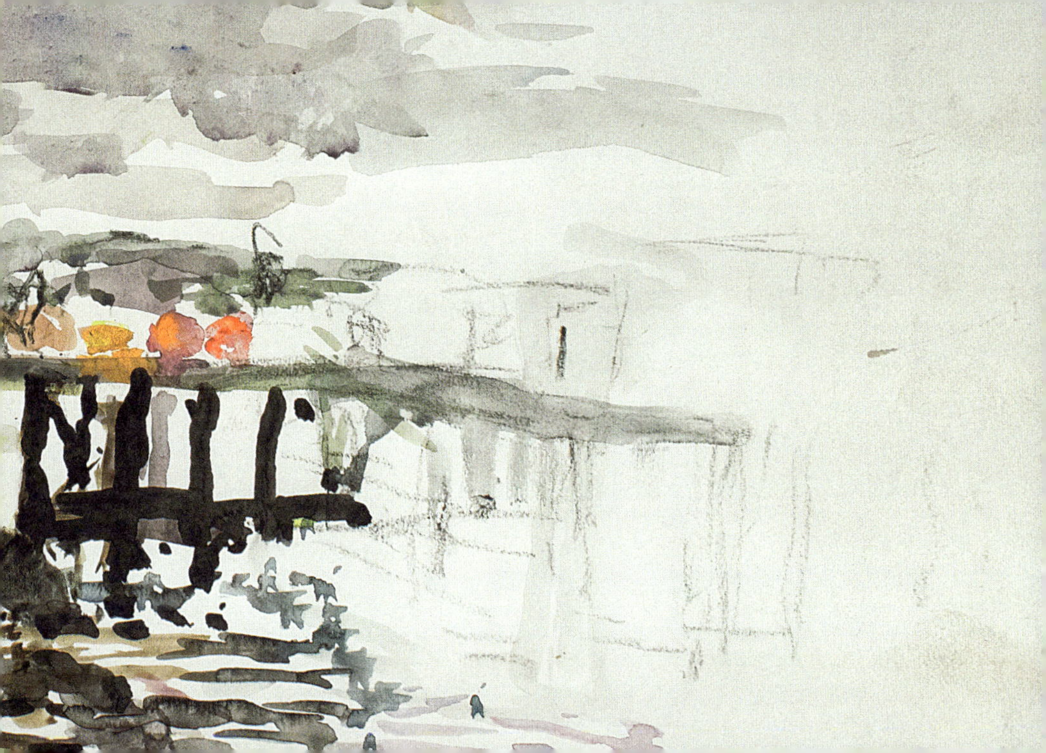

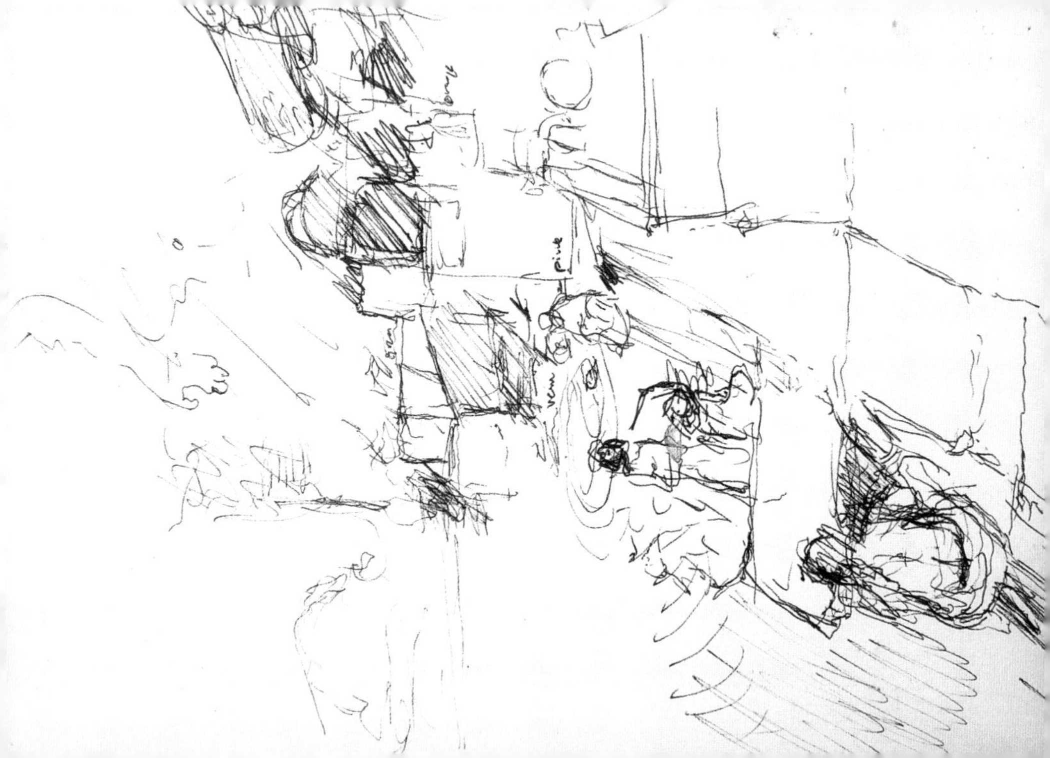

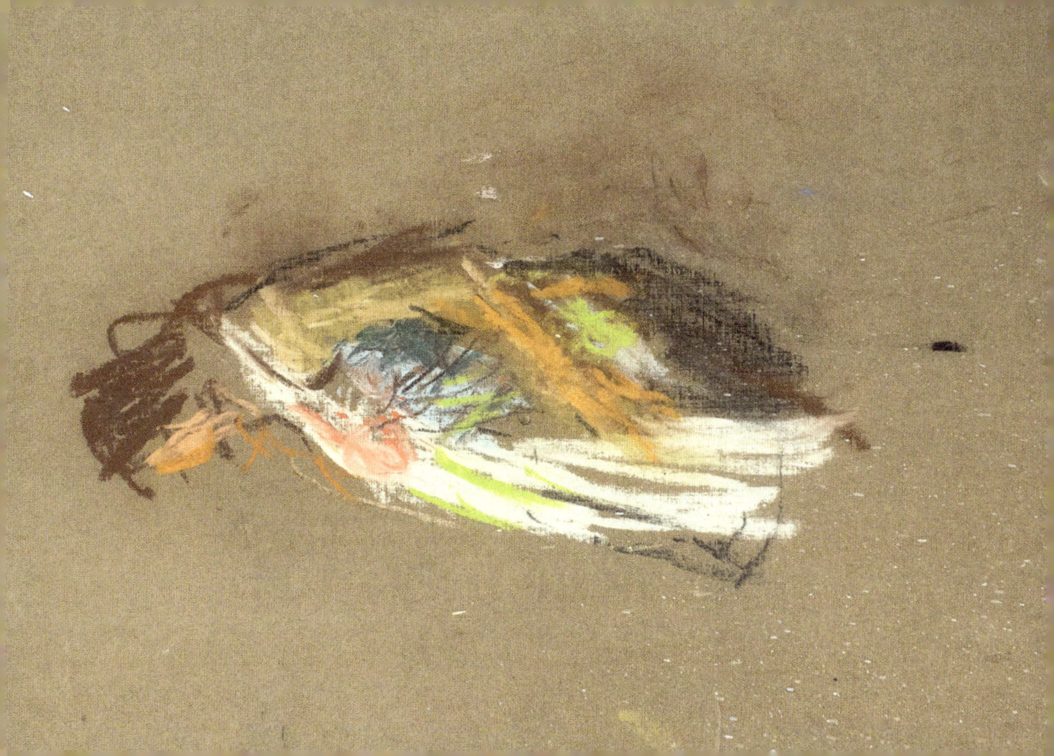

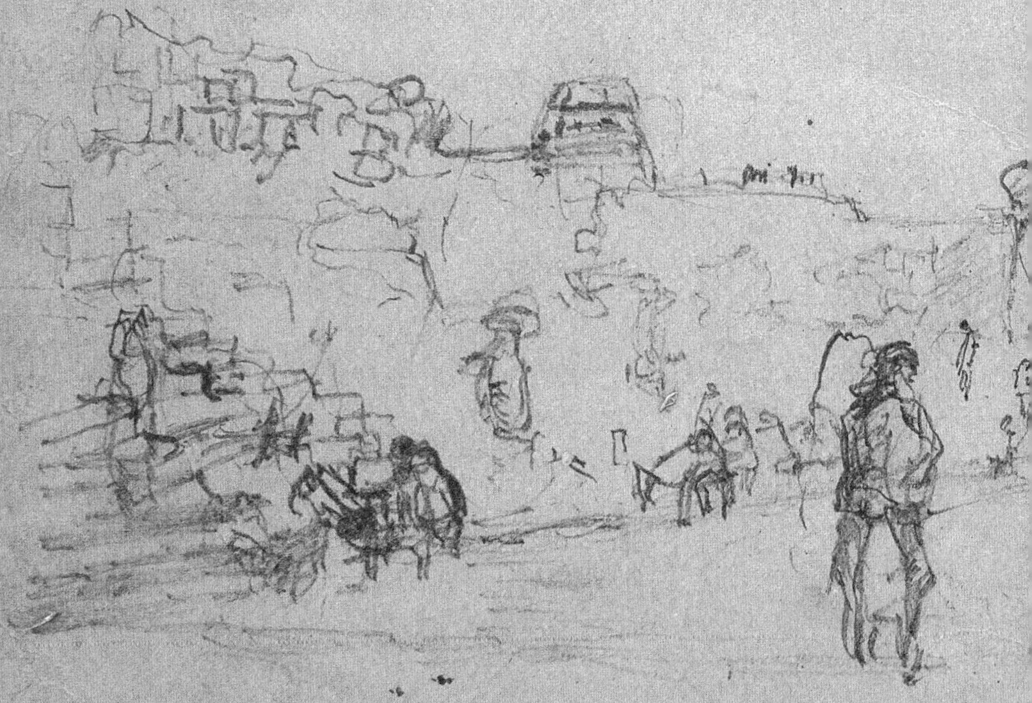

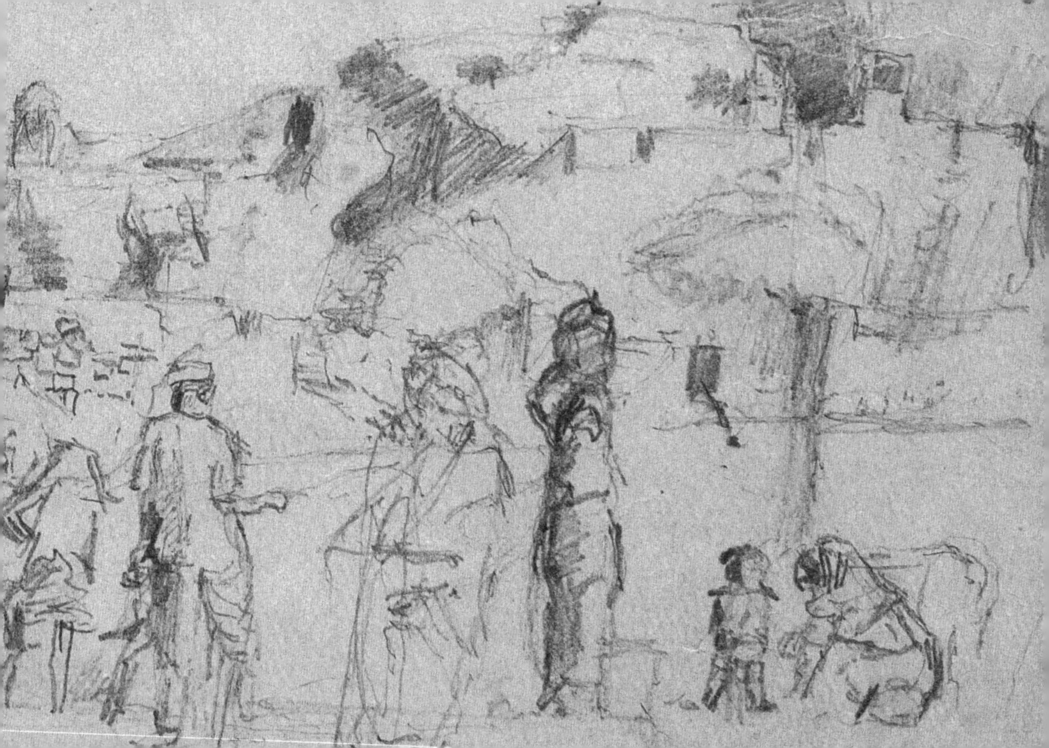

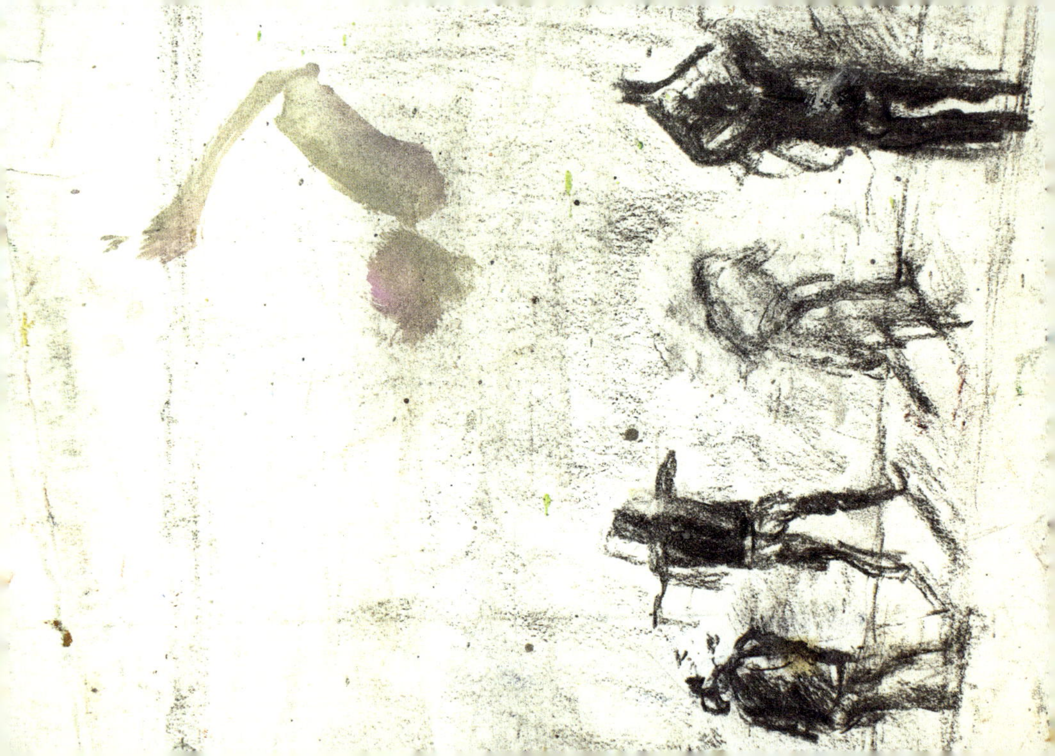

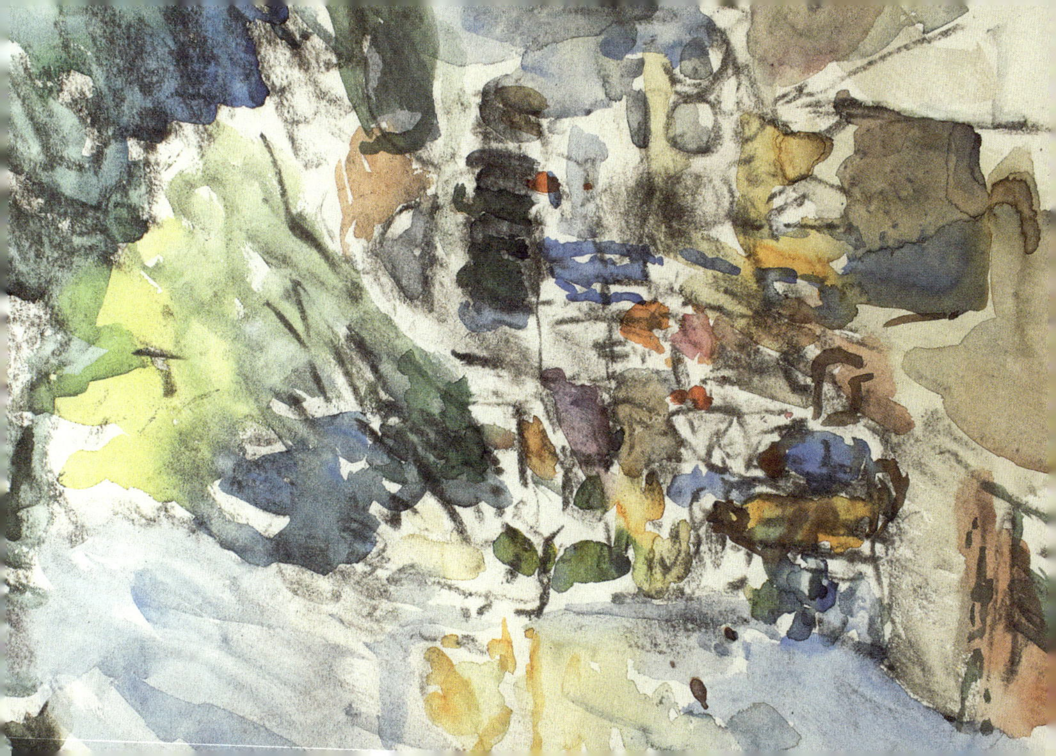

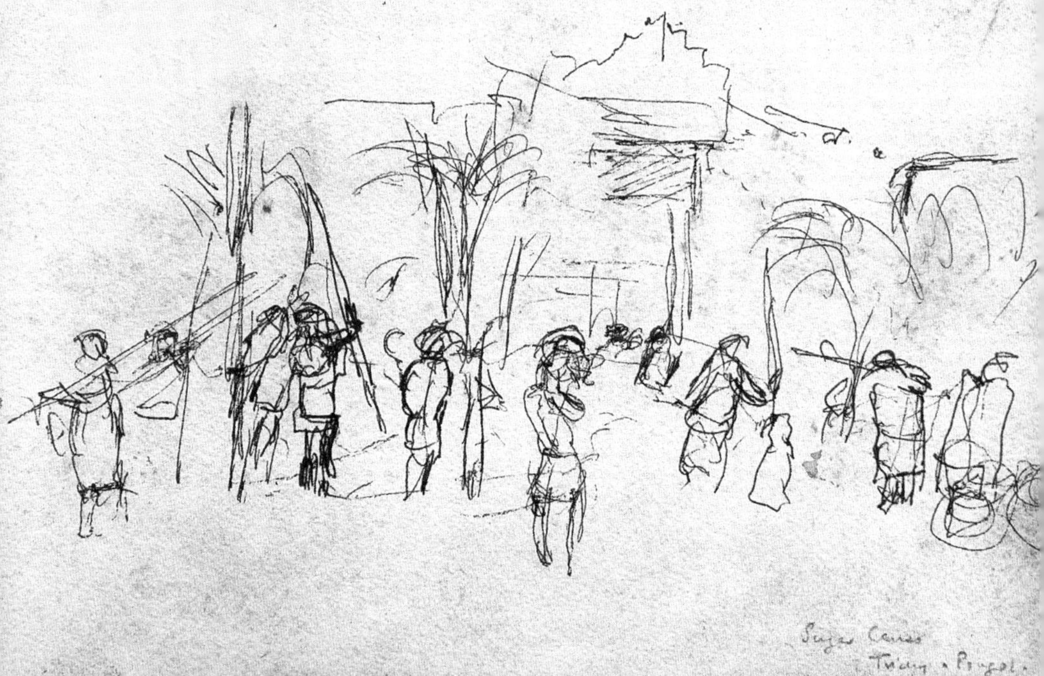

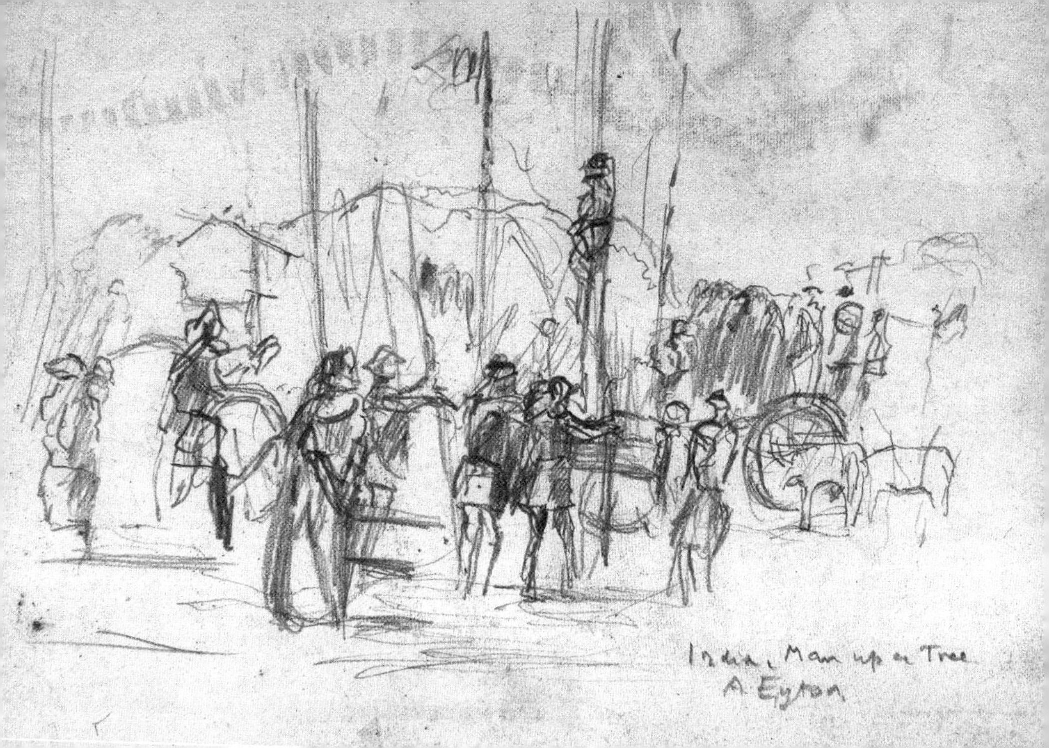
India, Man up a Tree
A. Eyton

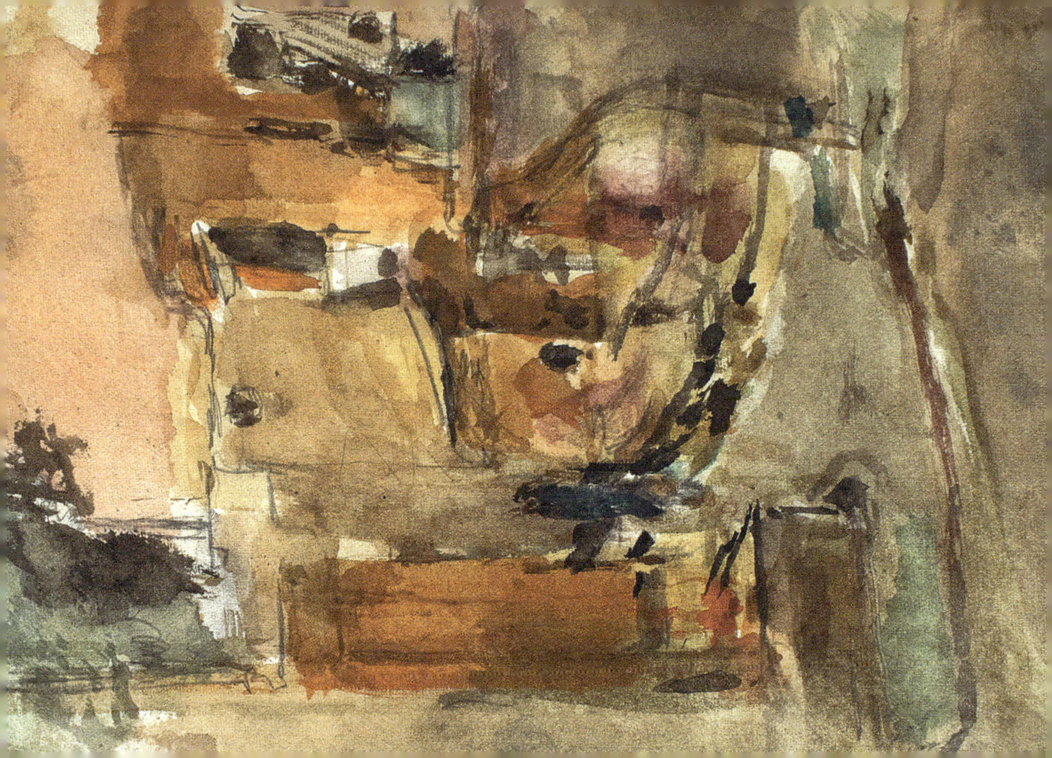

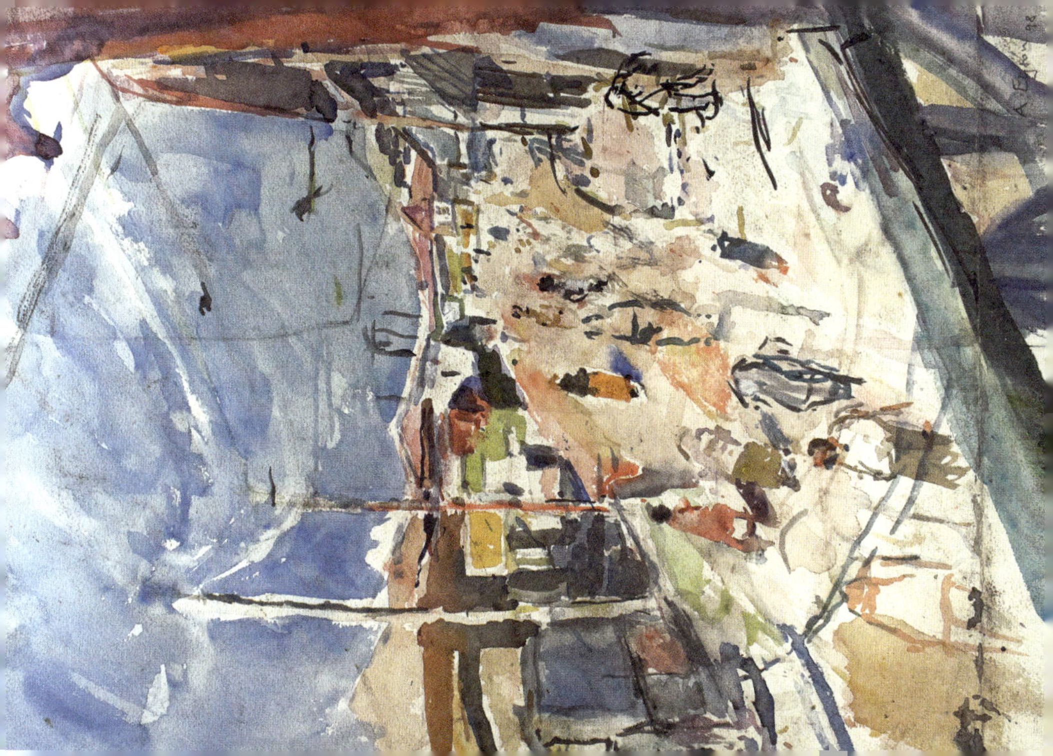

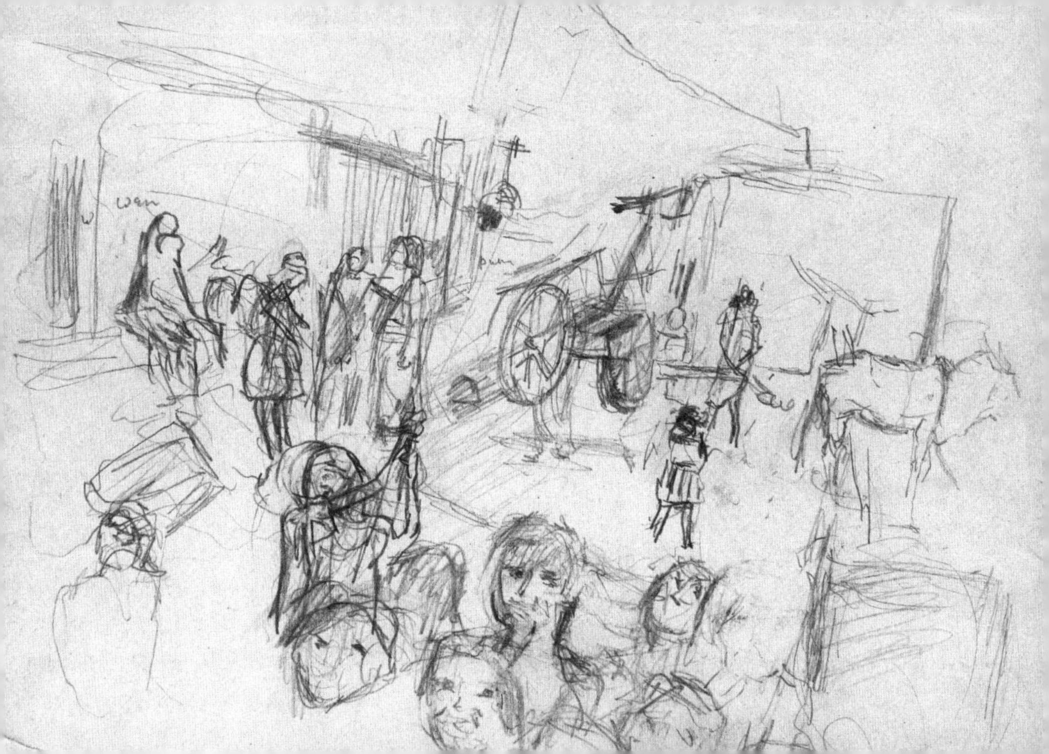

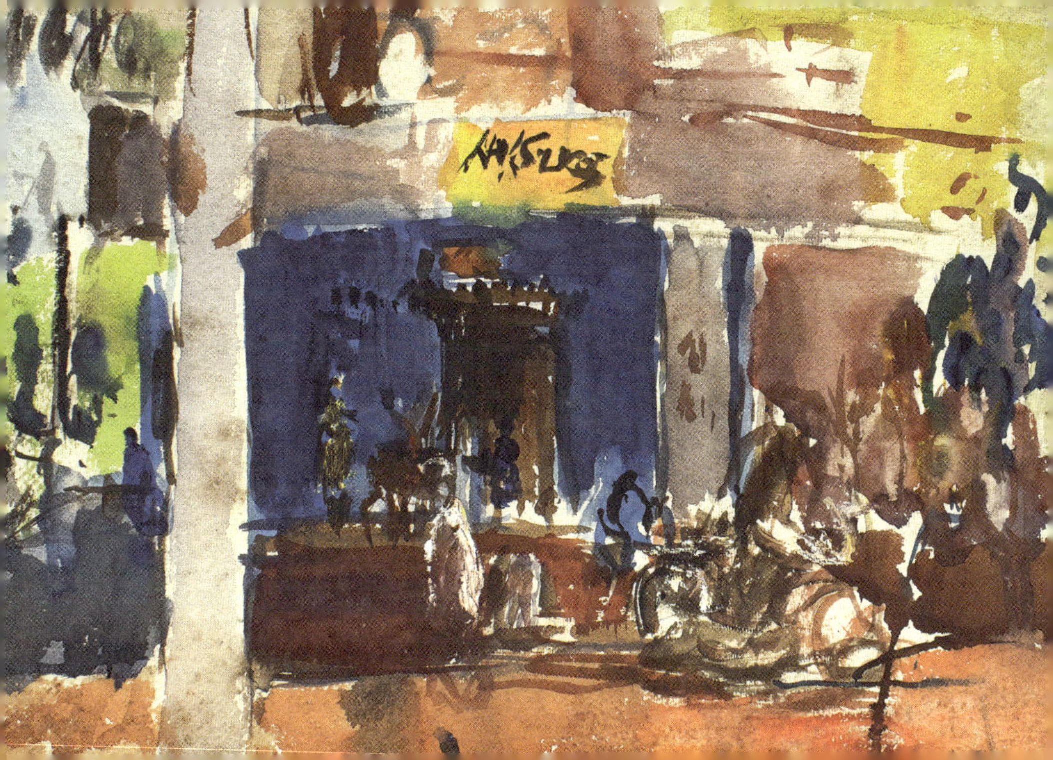

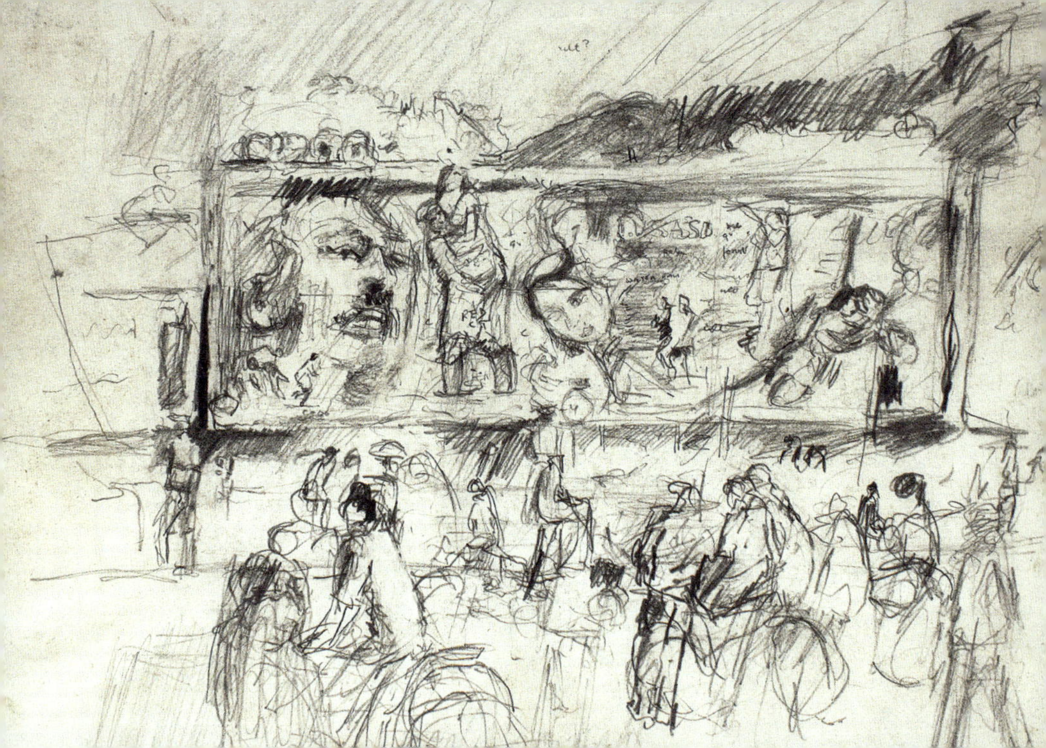

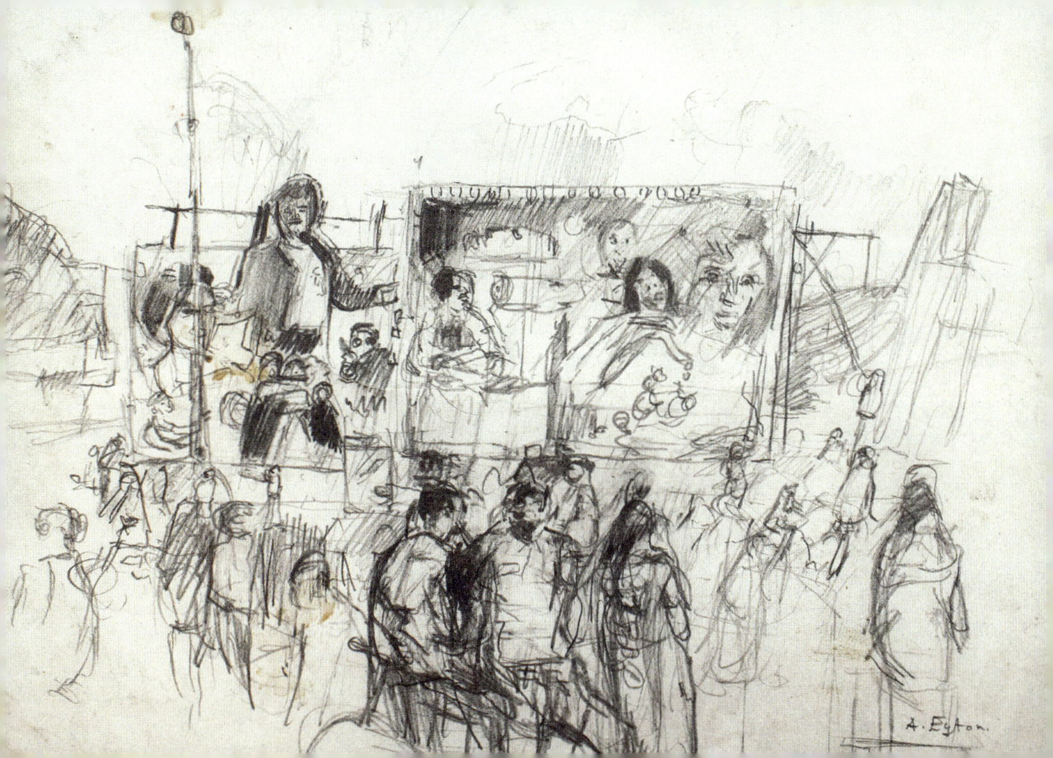
A. Eyton.

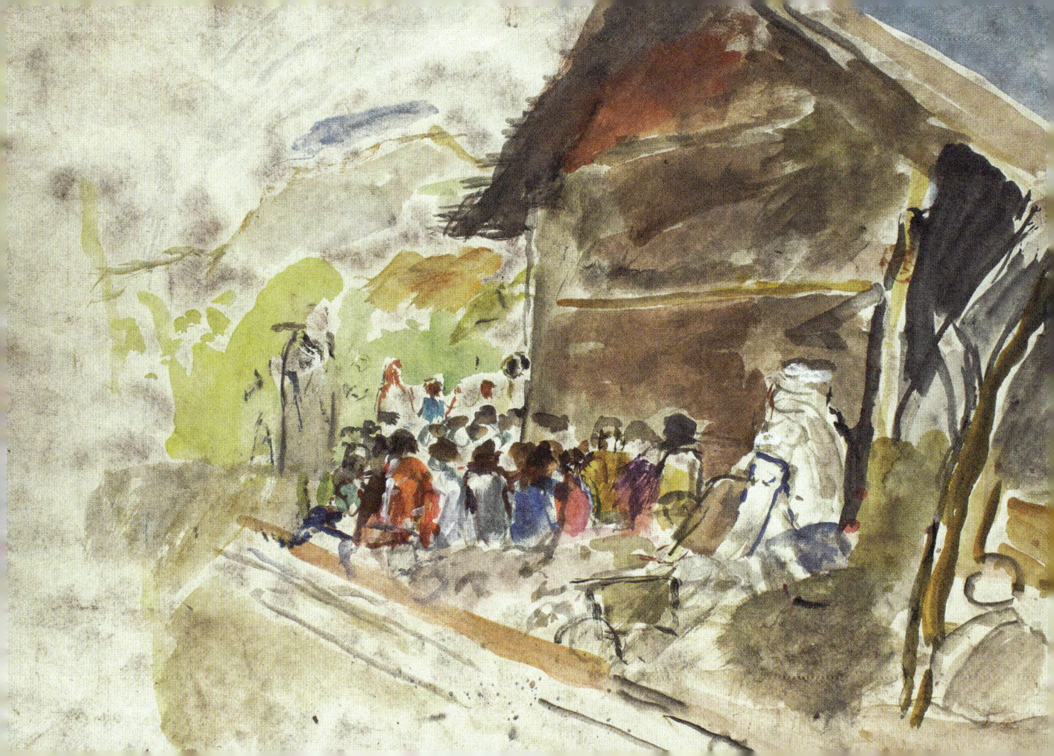

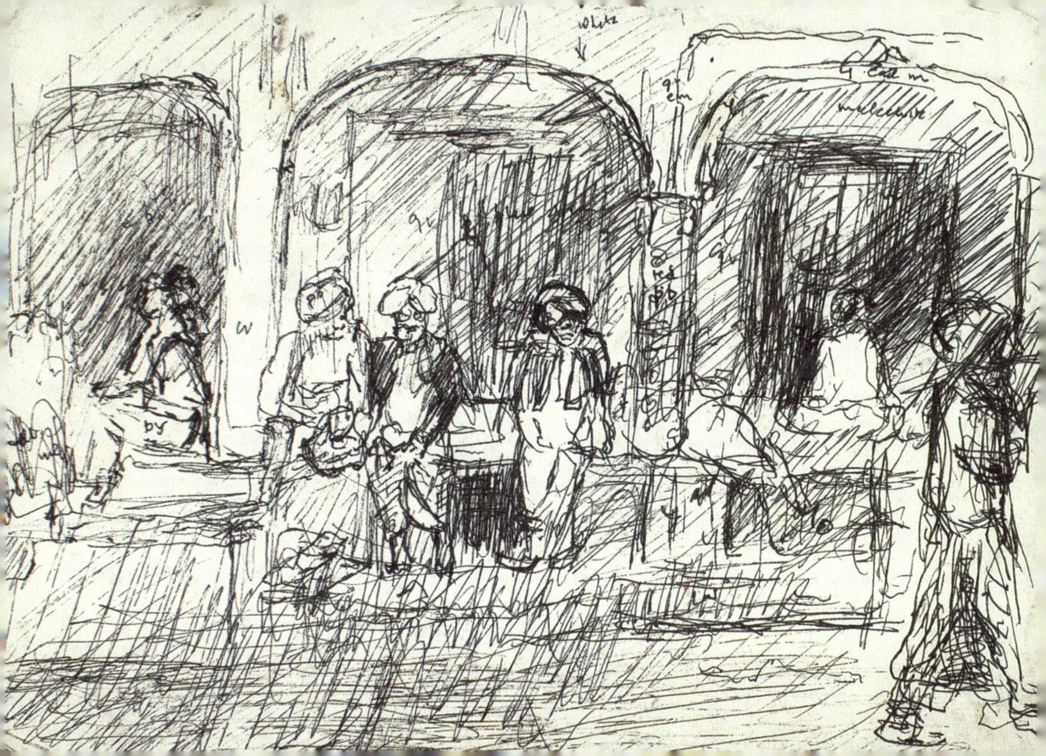

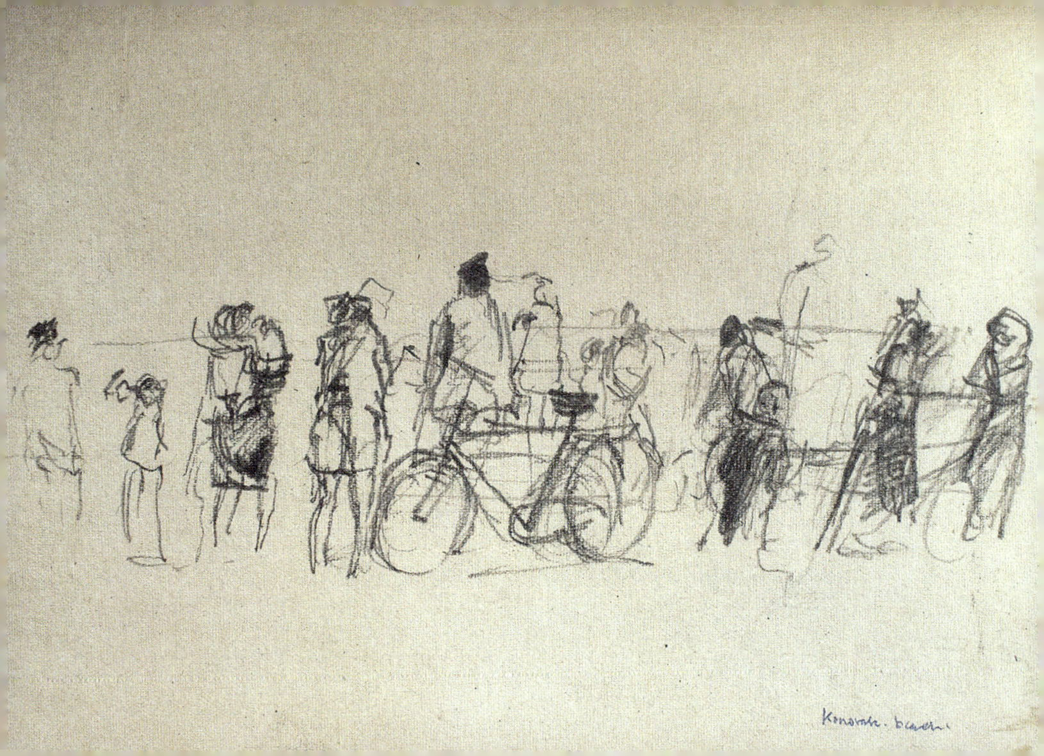

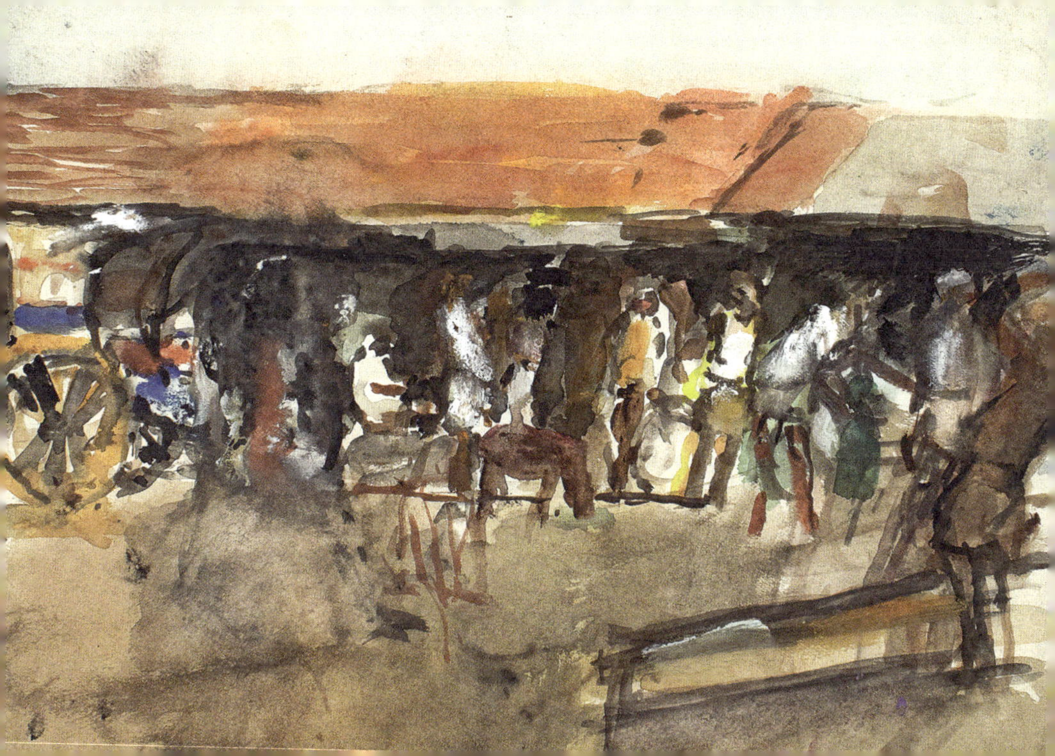

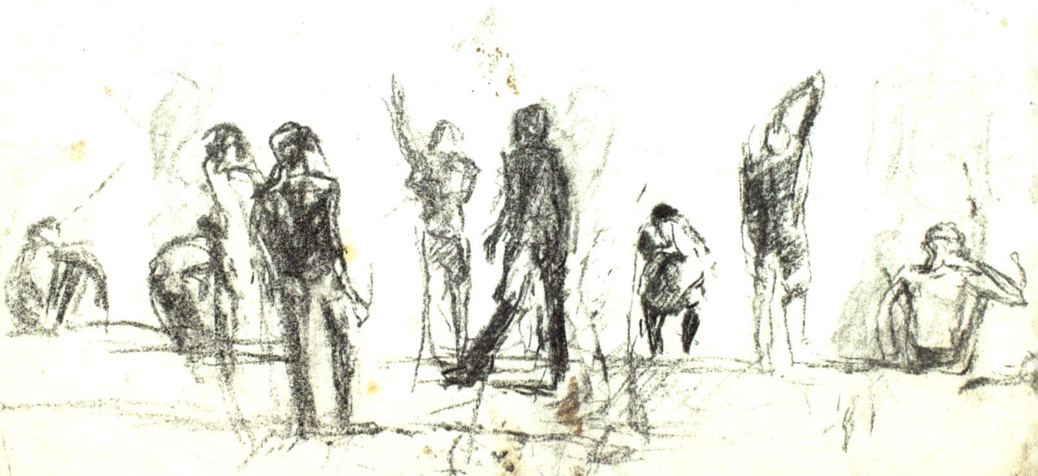

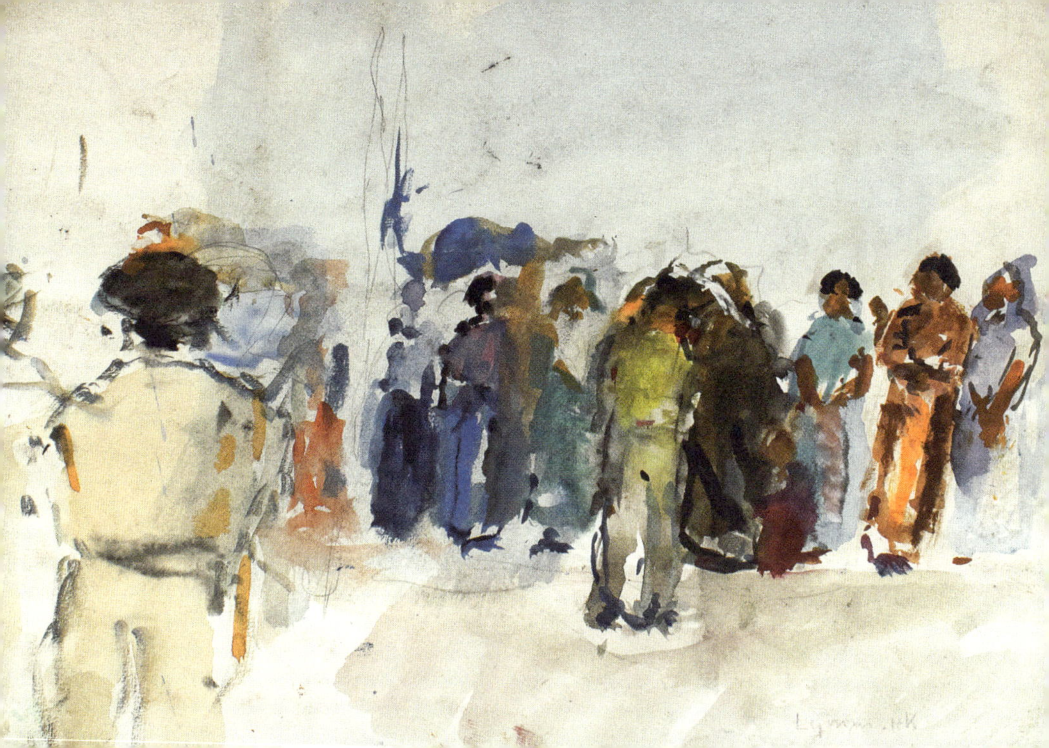

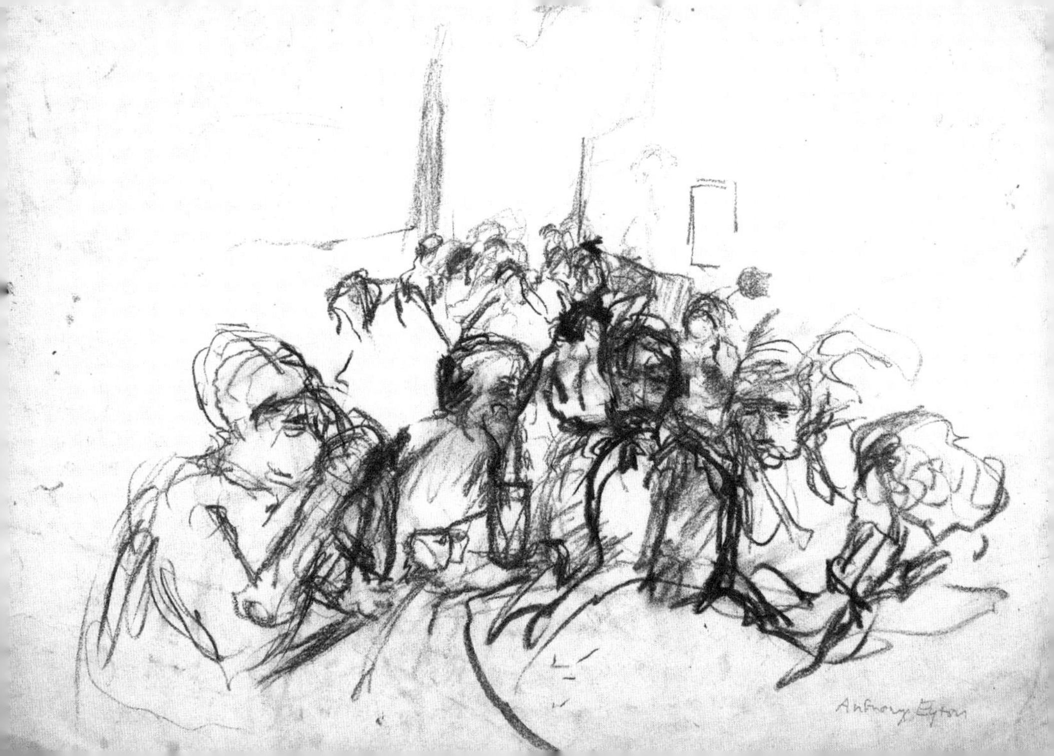
Anthony Eyton

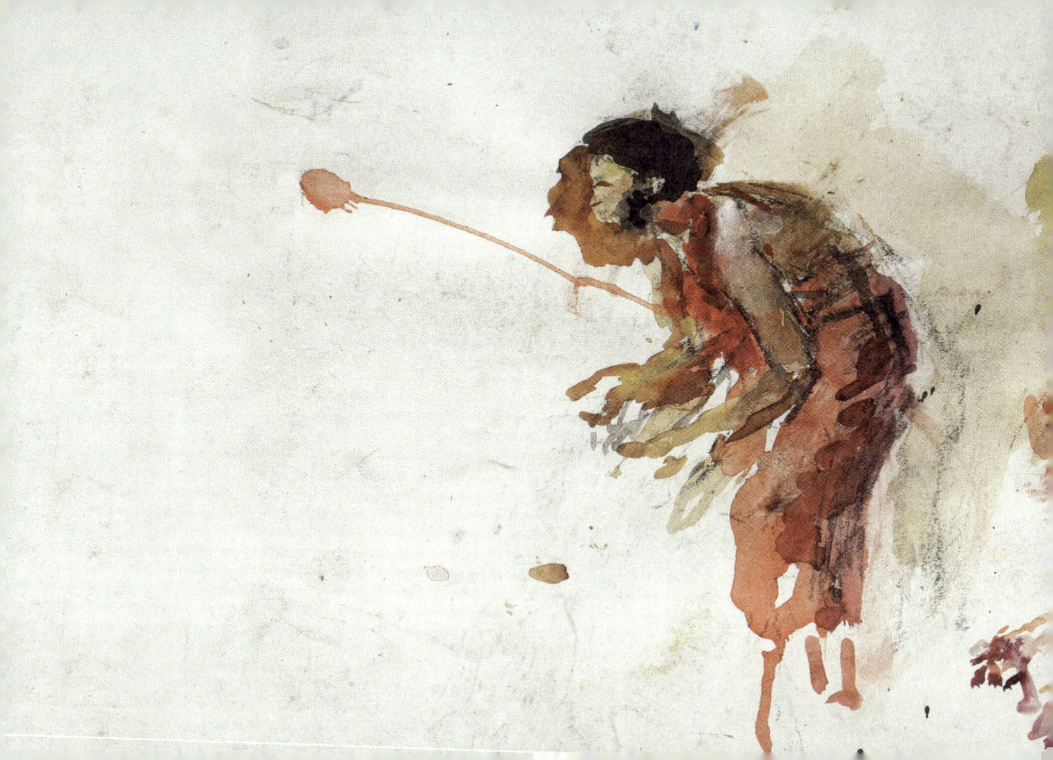

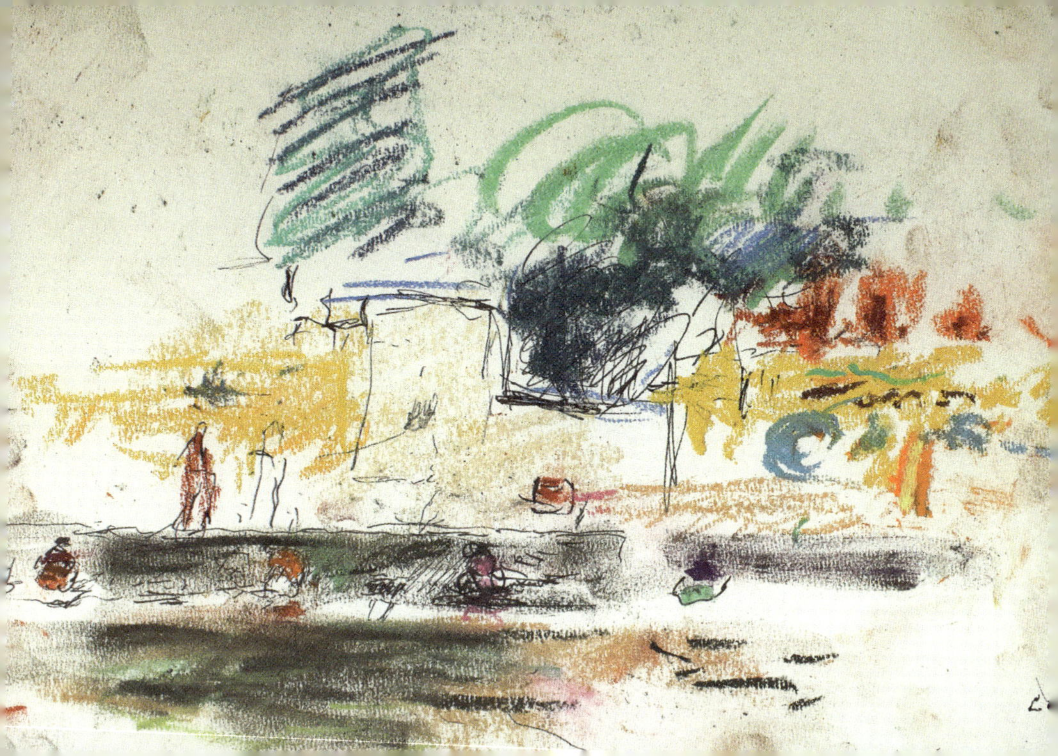

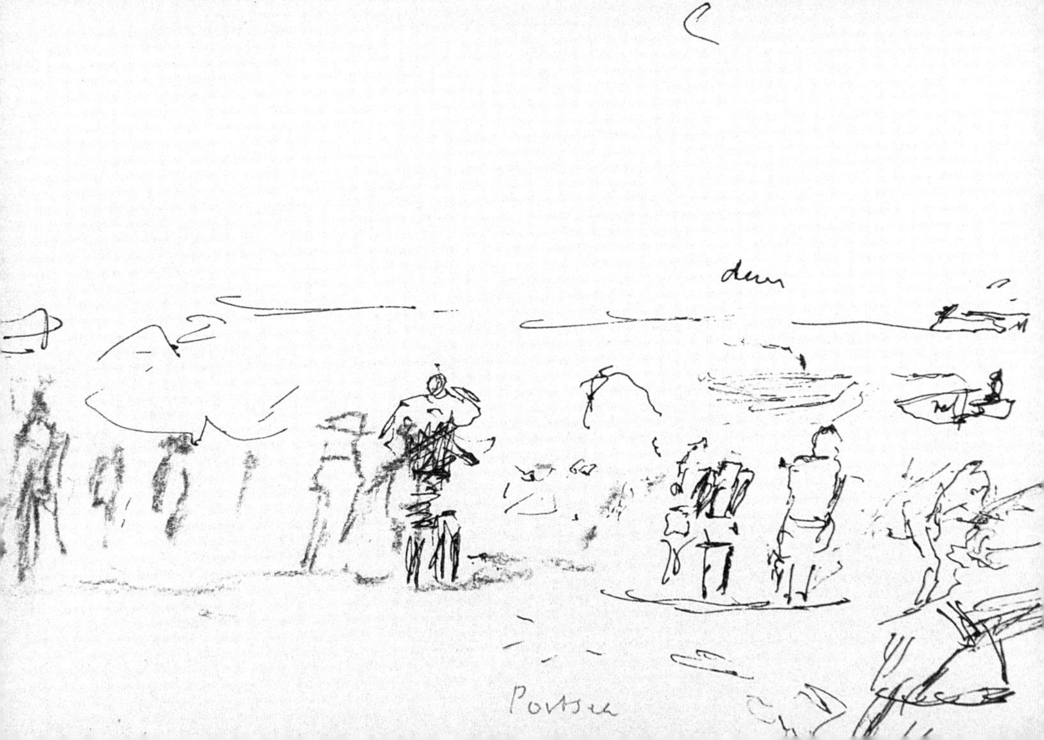
Portsea

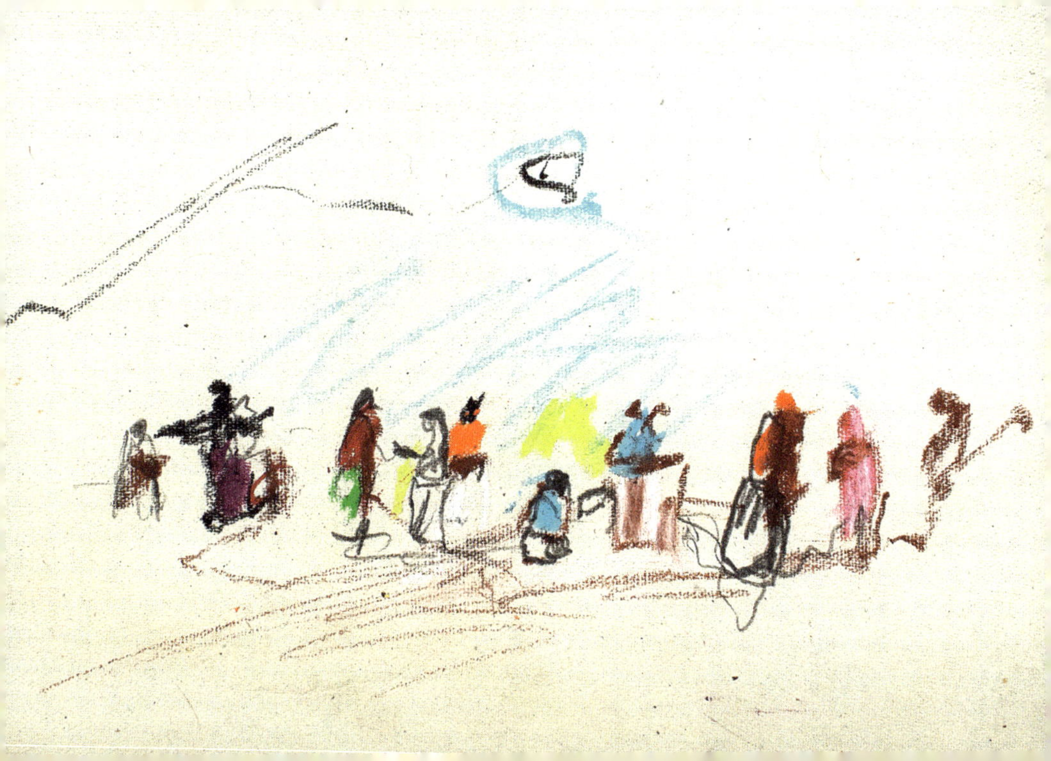

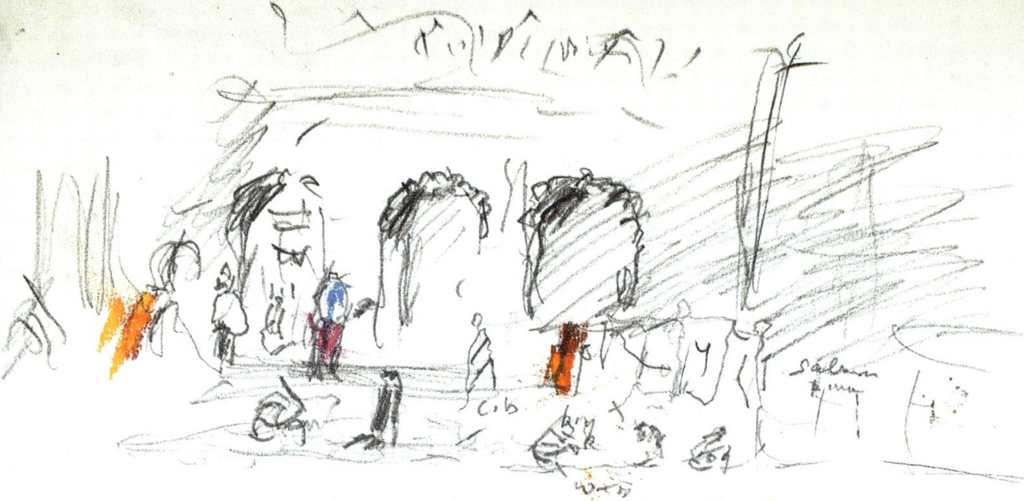

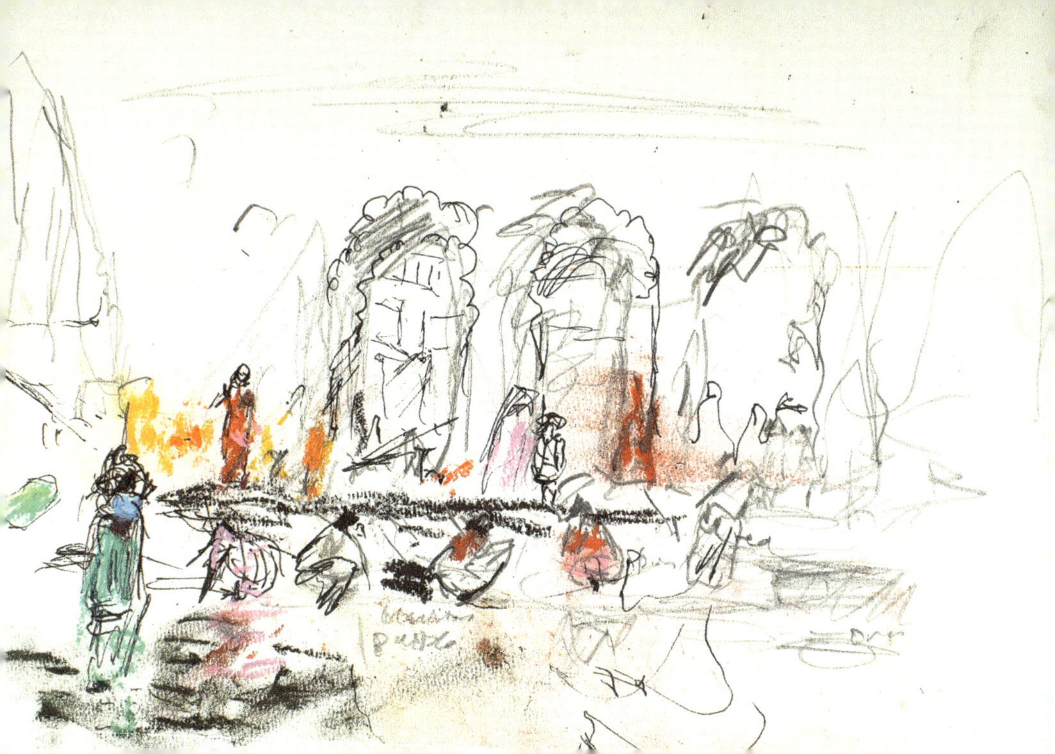

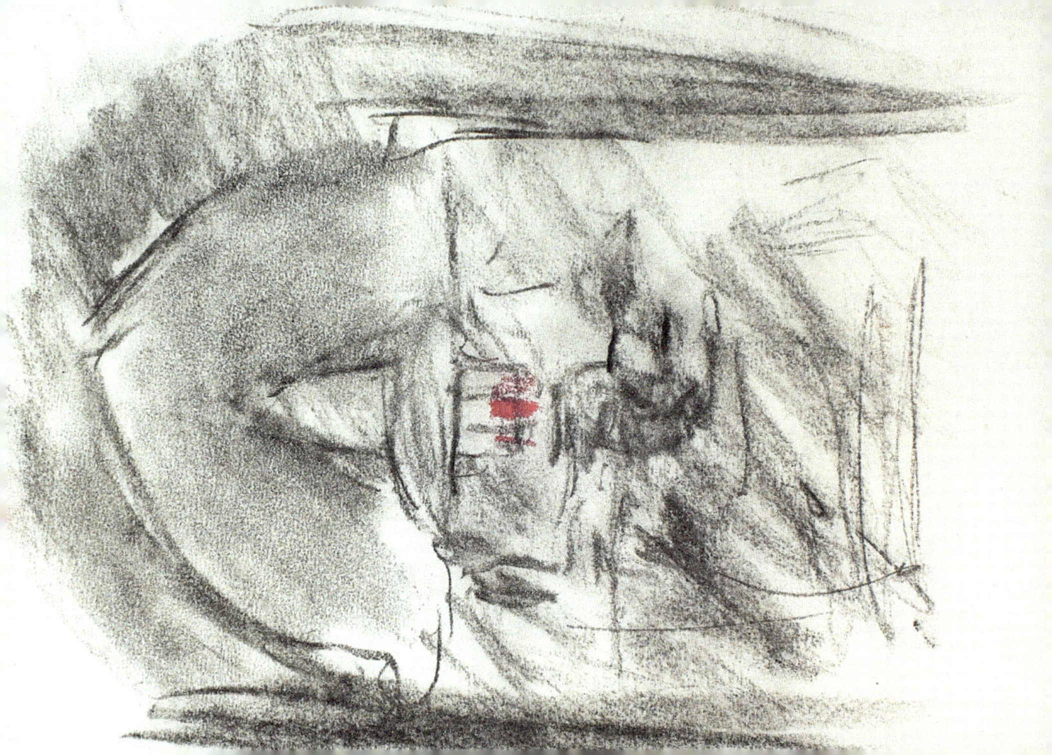

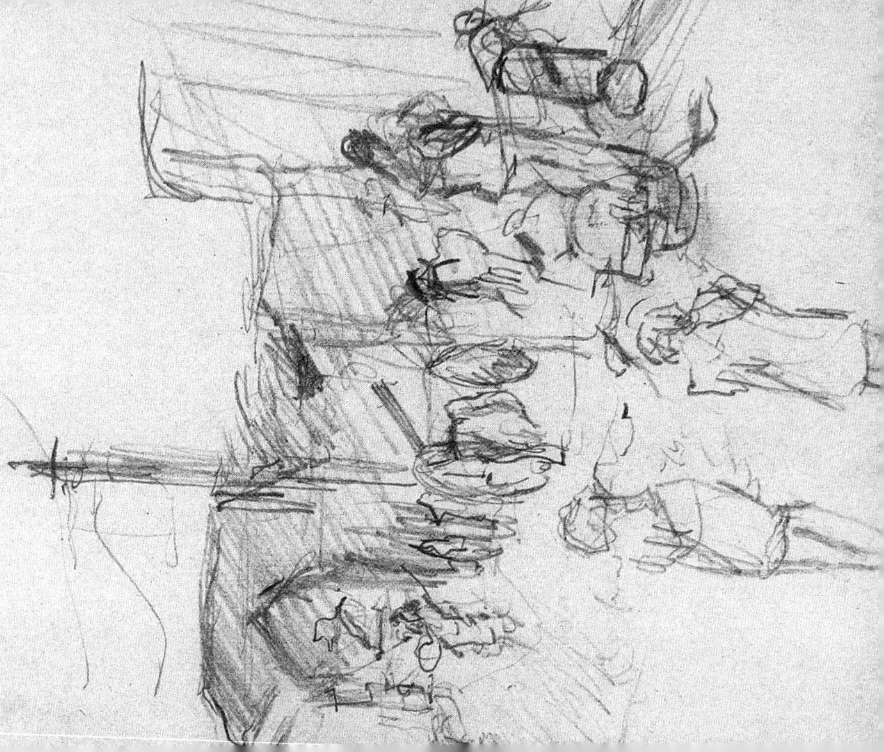

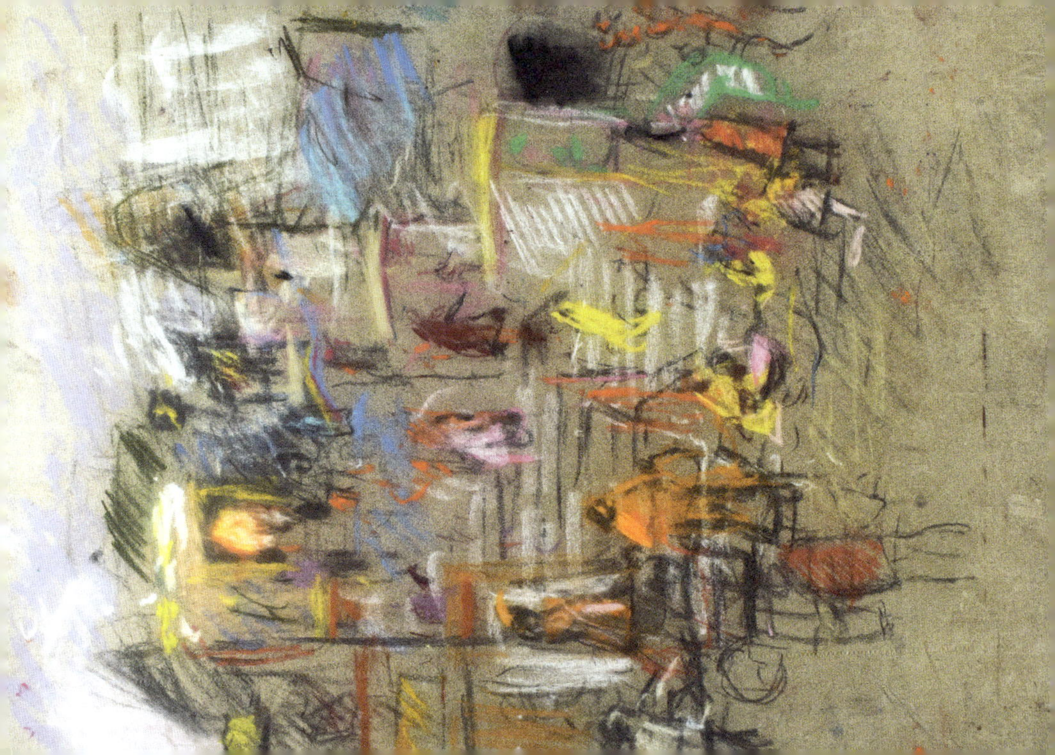

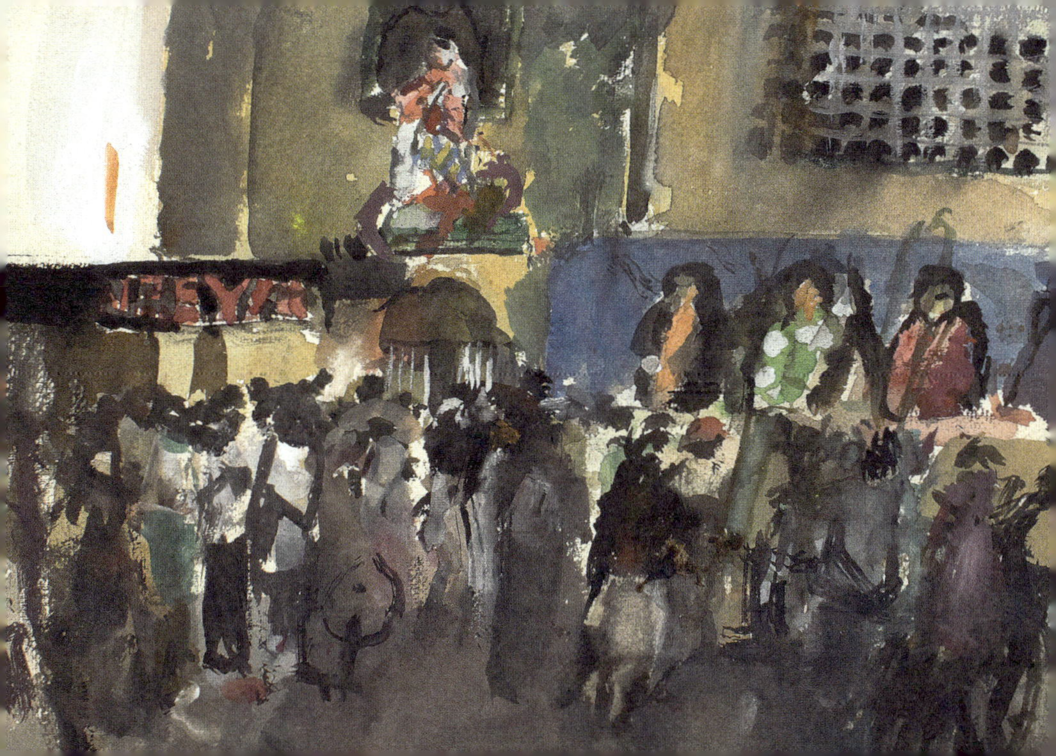

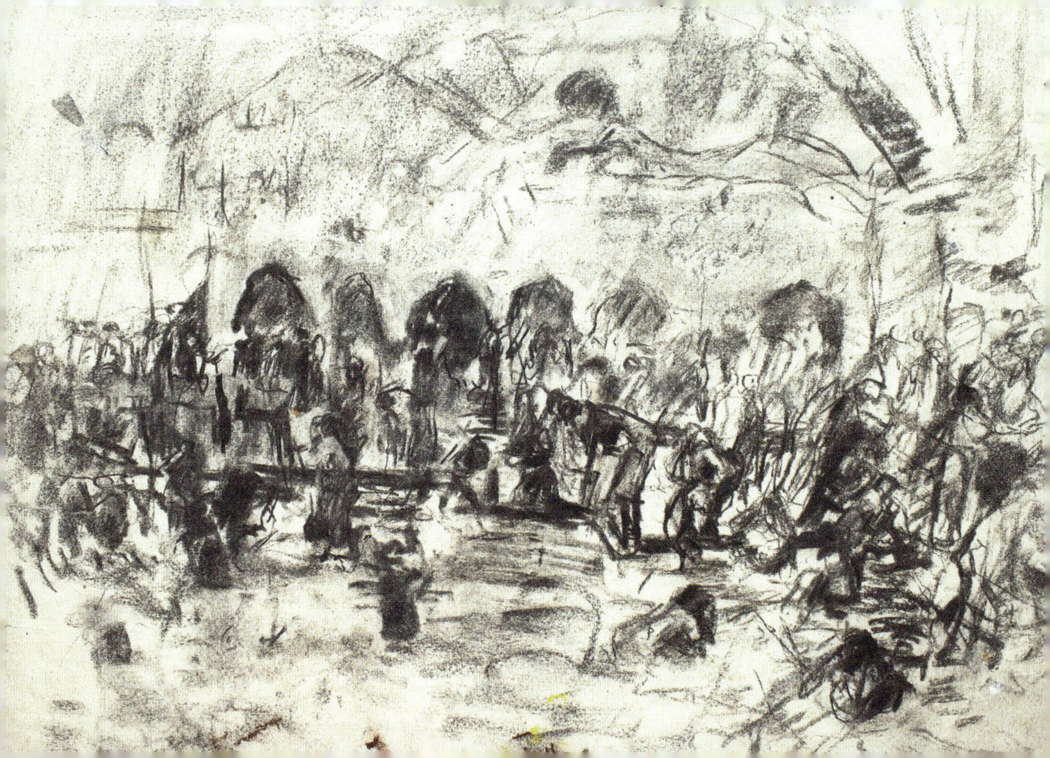

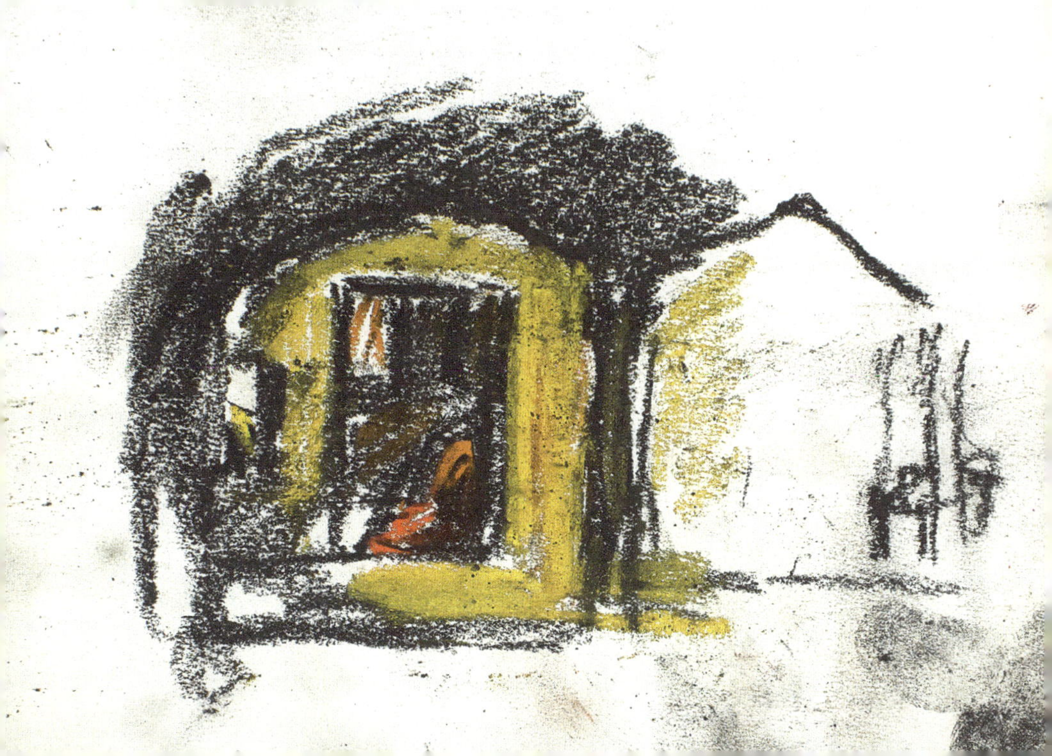

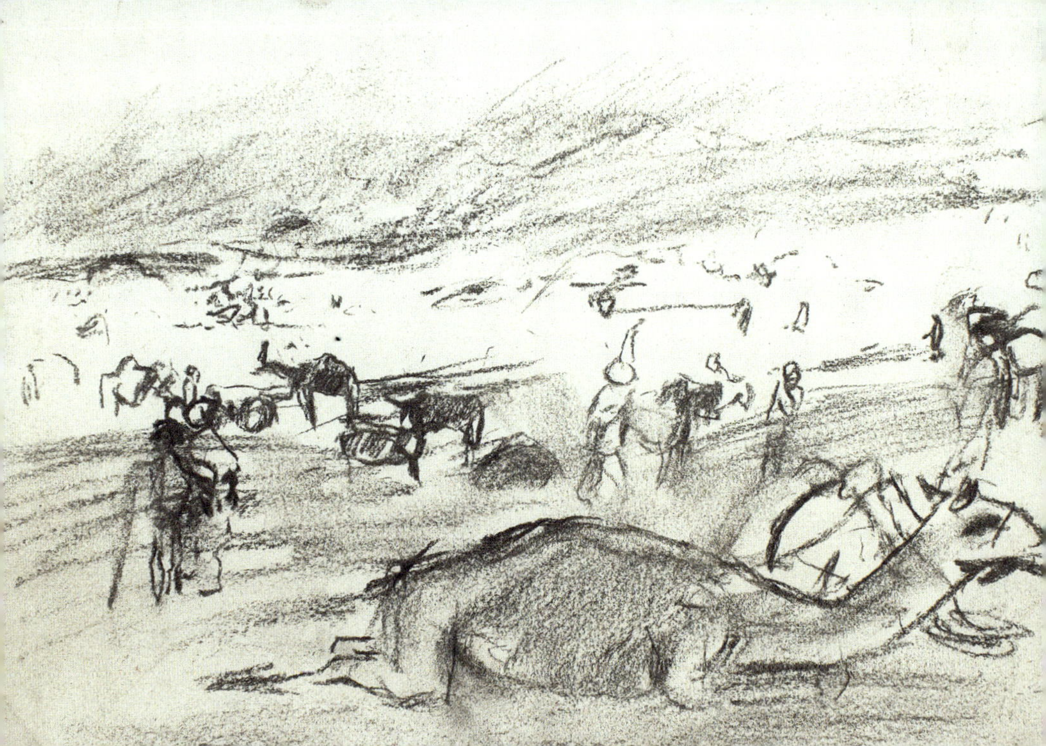

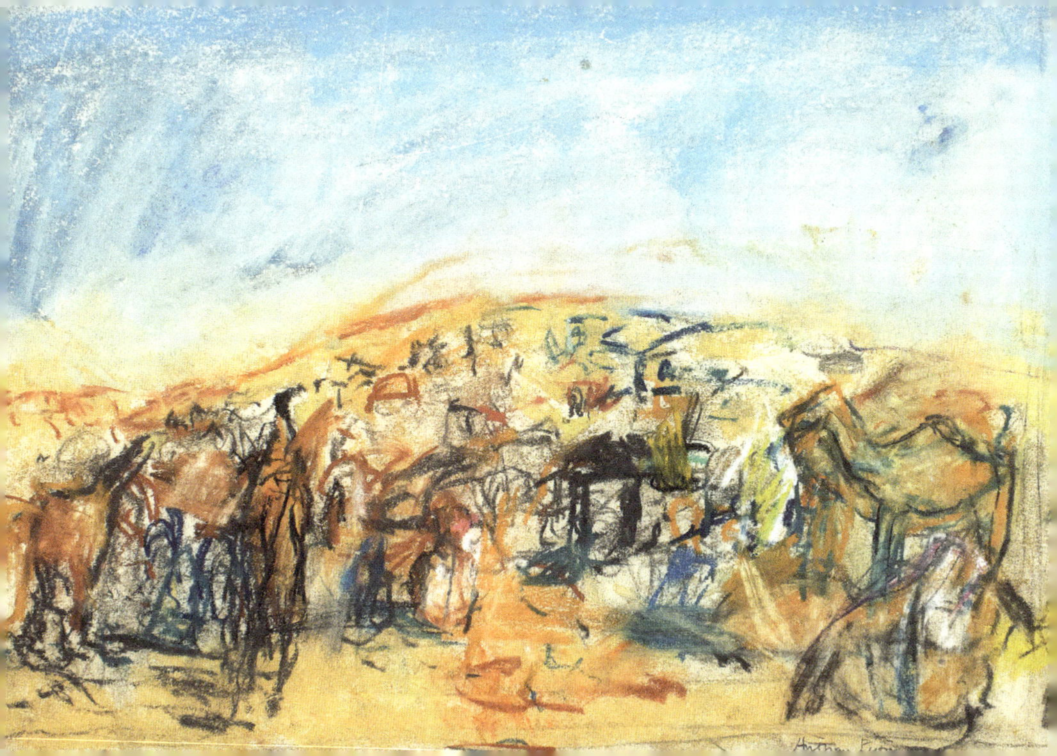

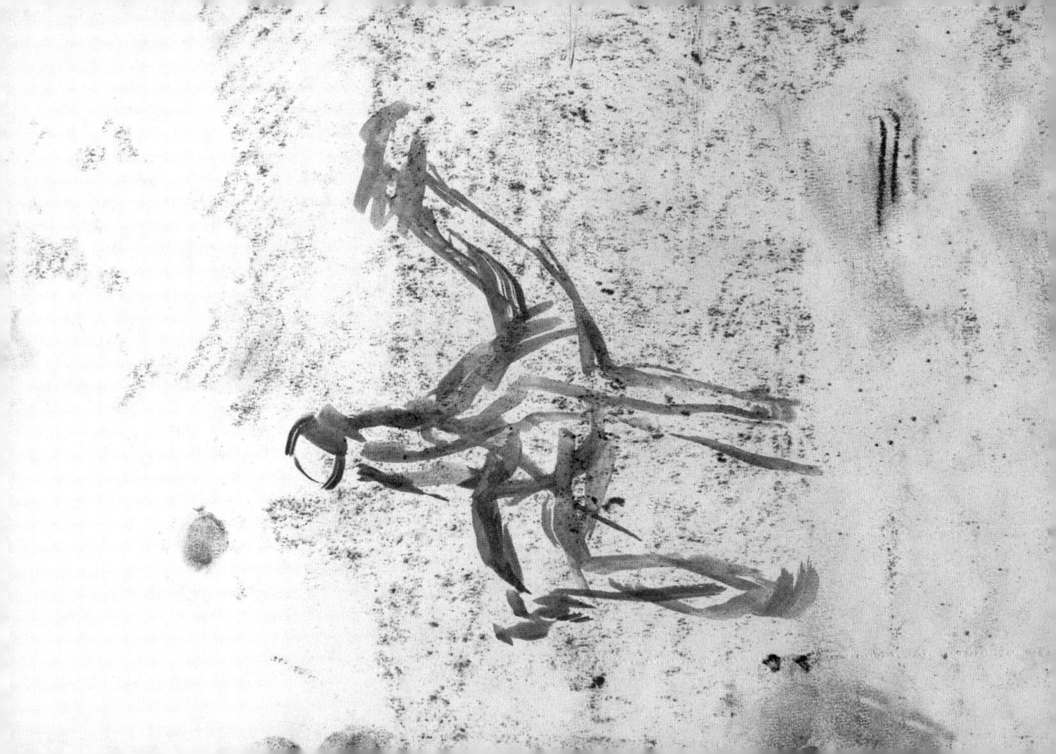

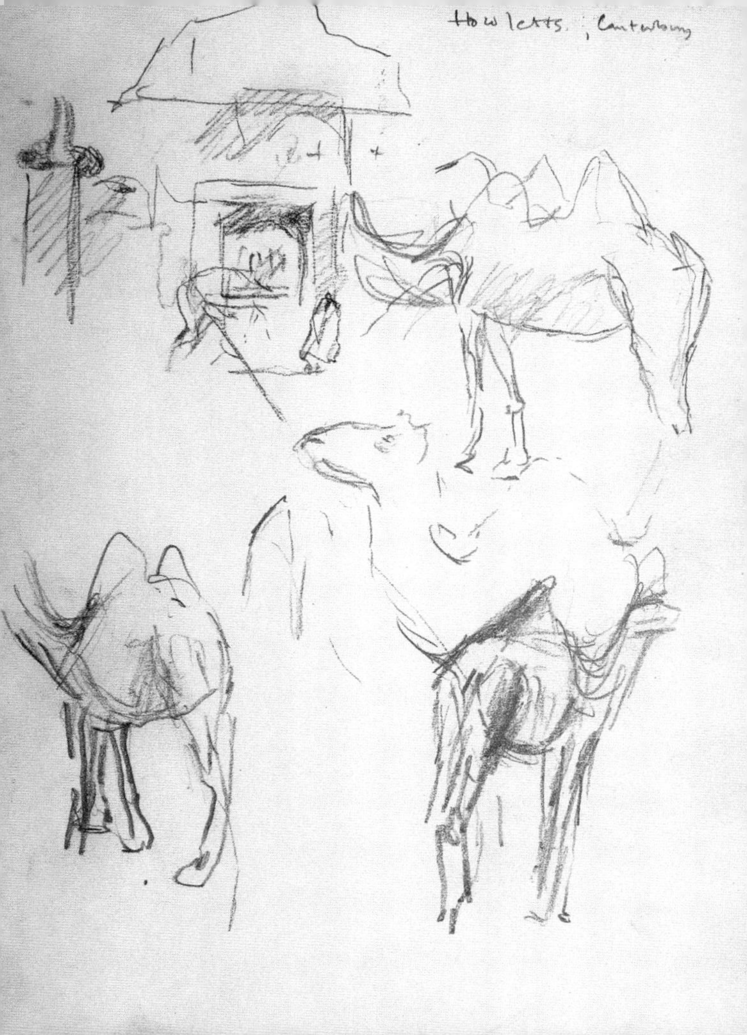
Howletts, Canterbury

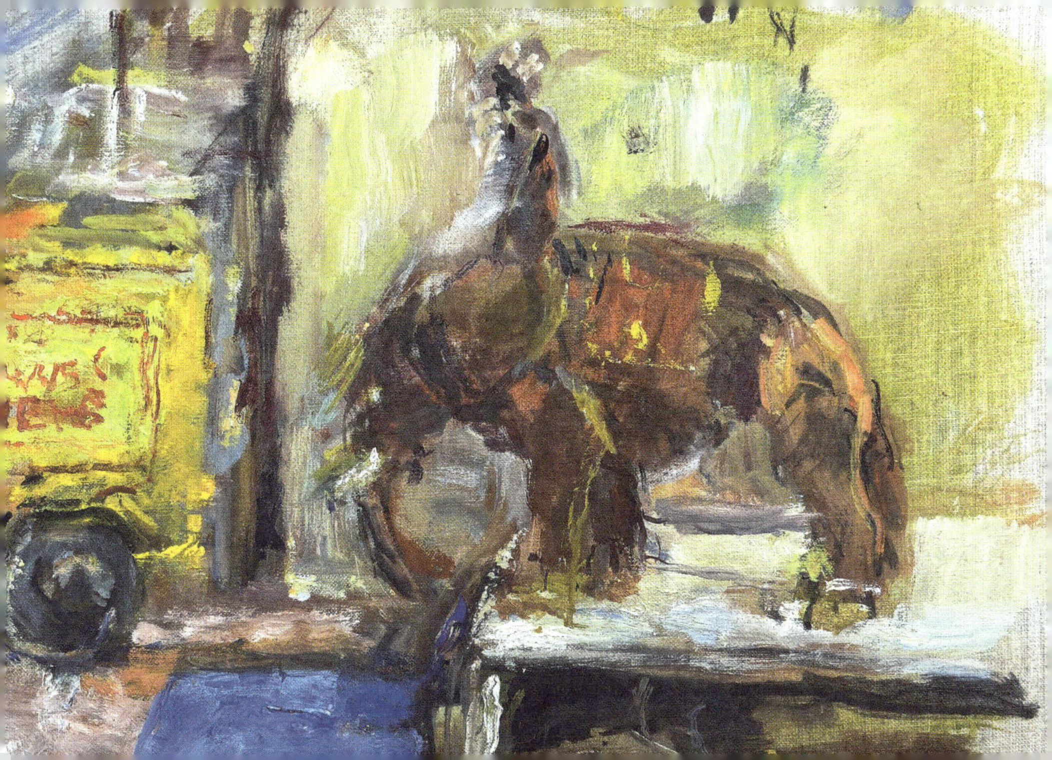

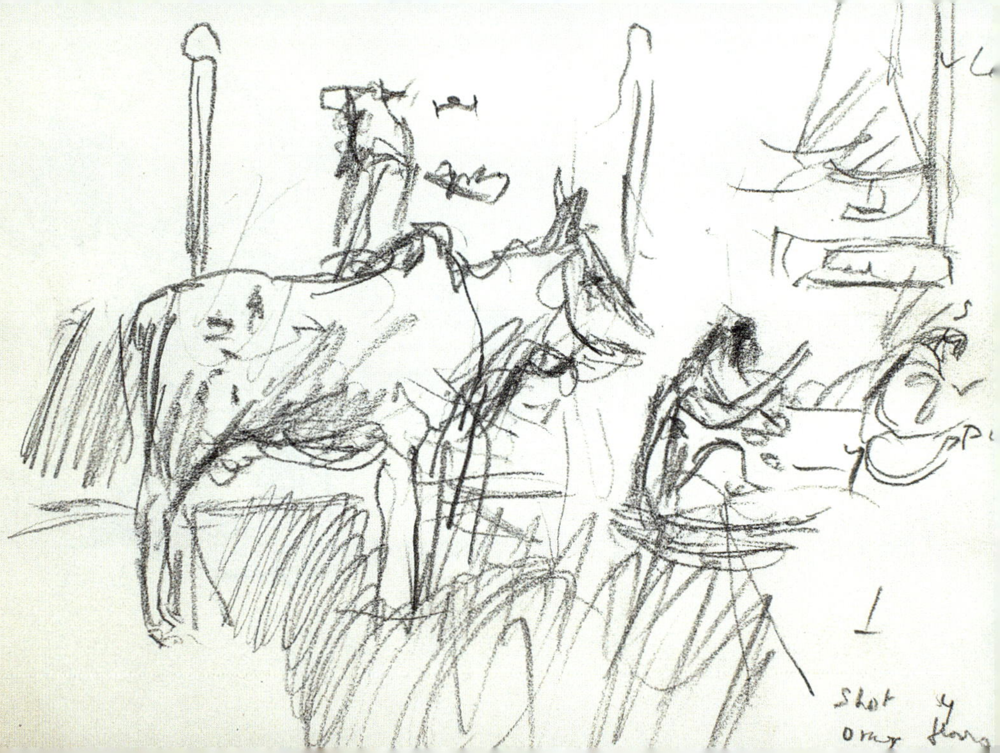
Shot

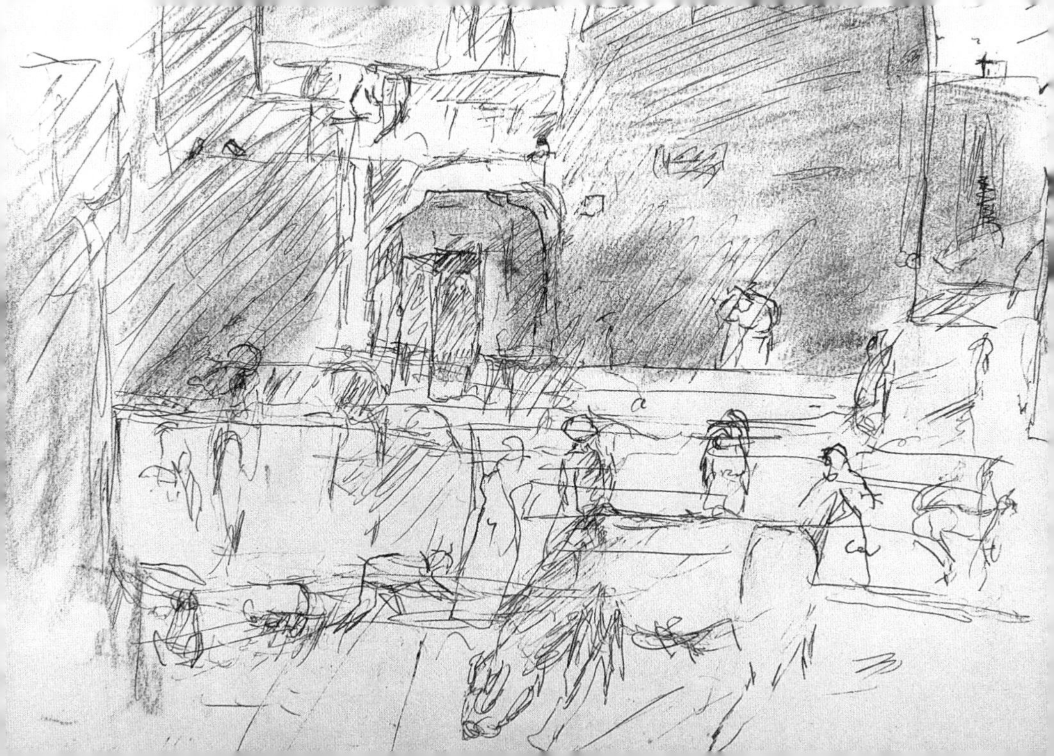

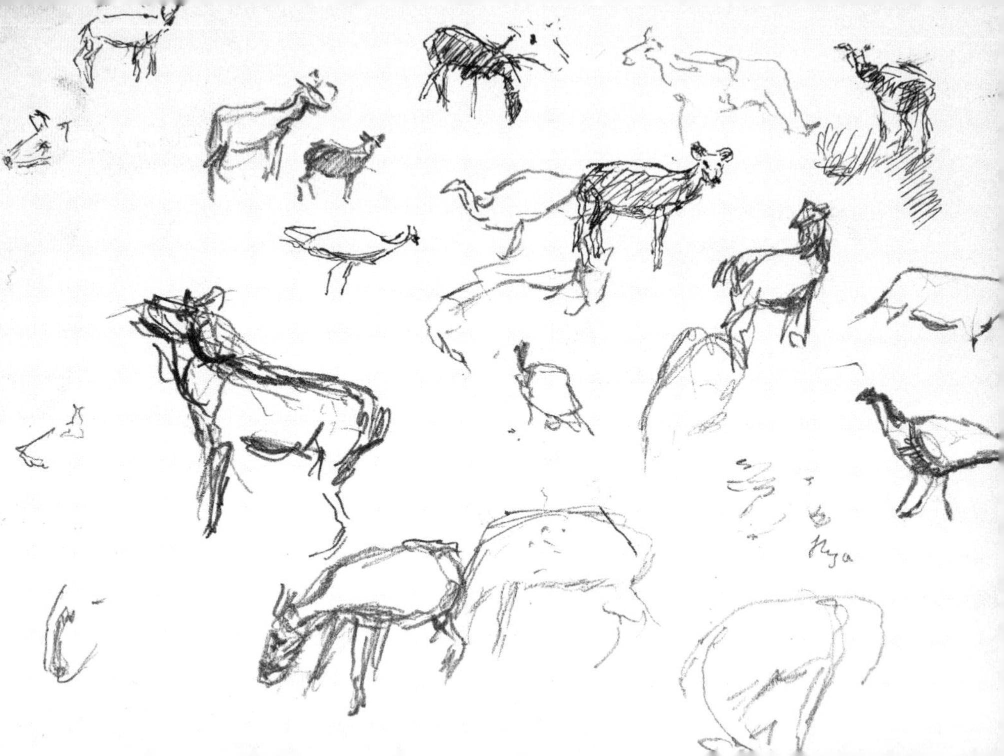

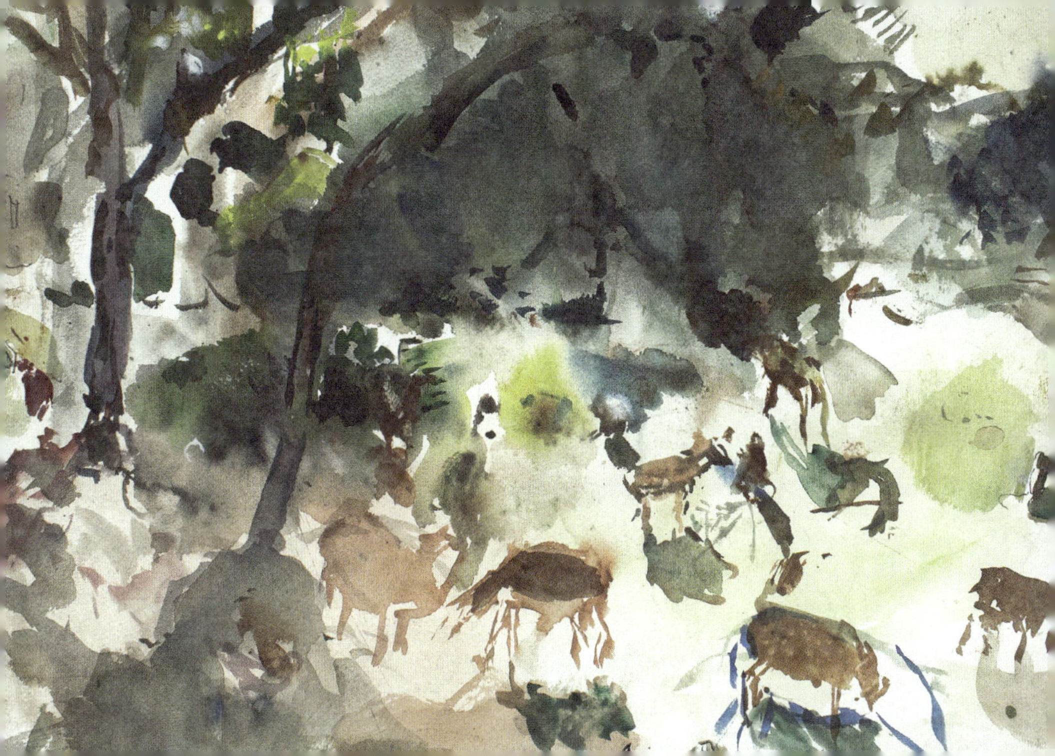

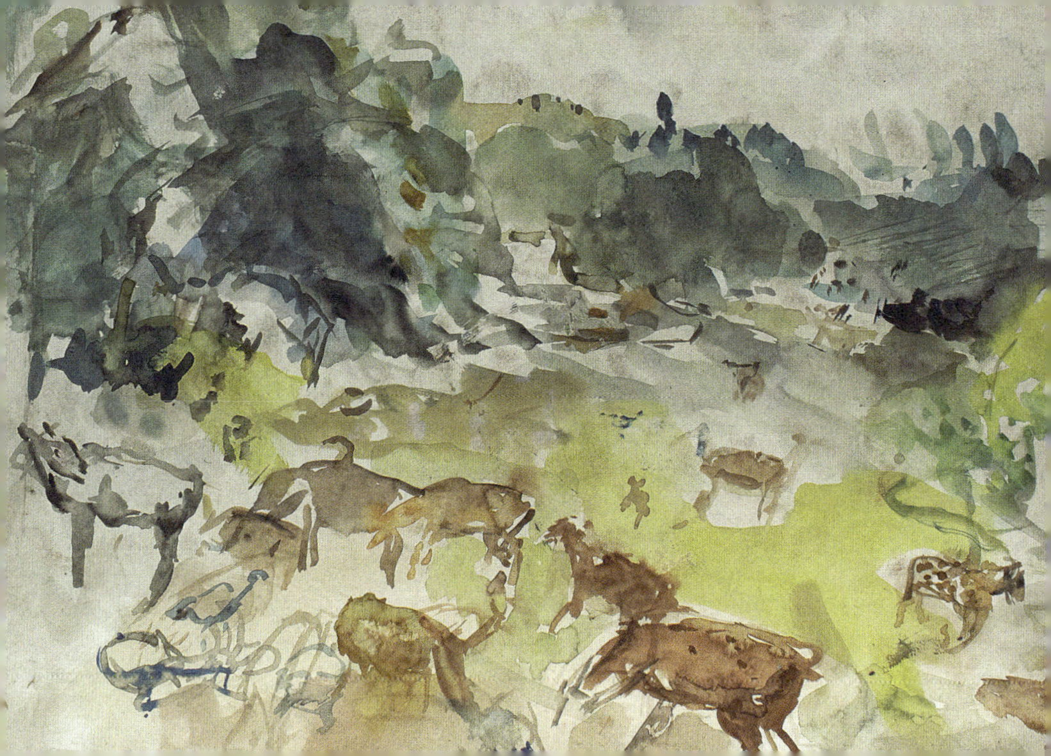

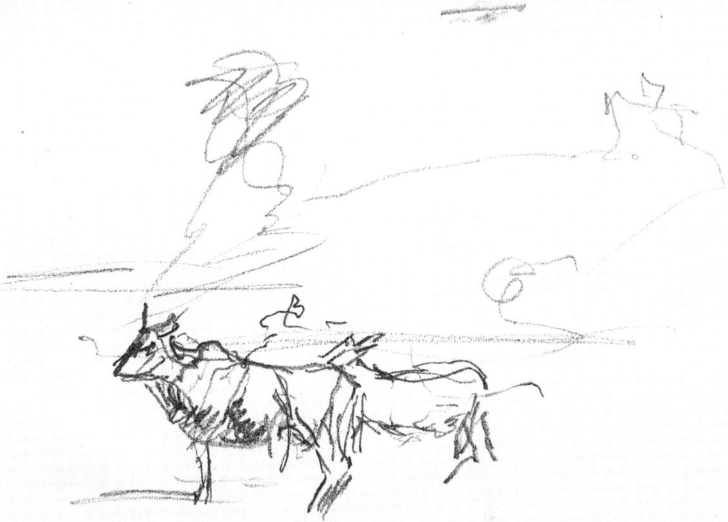

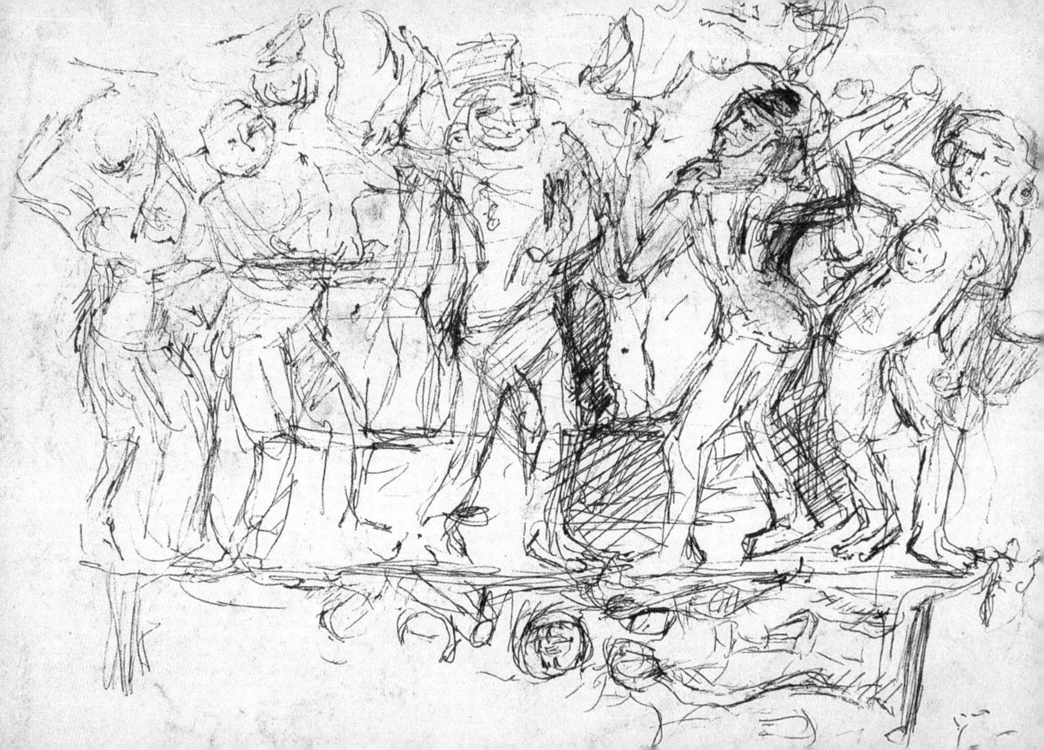

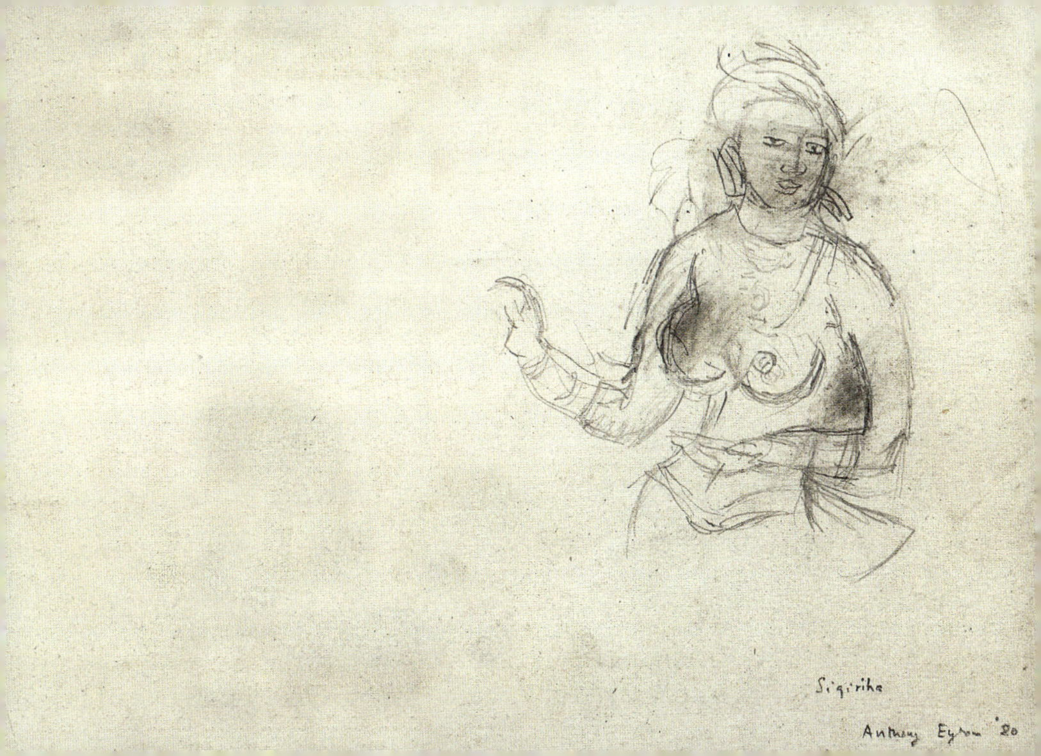
Sigiriha
Anthony Eyton '20

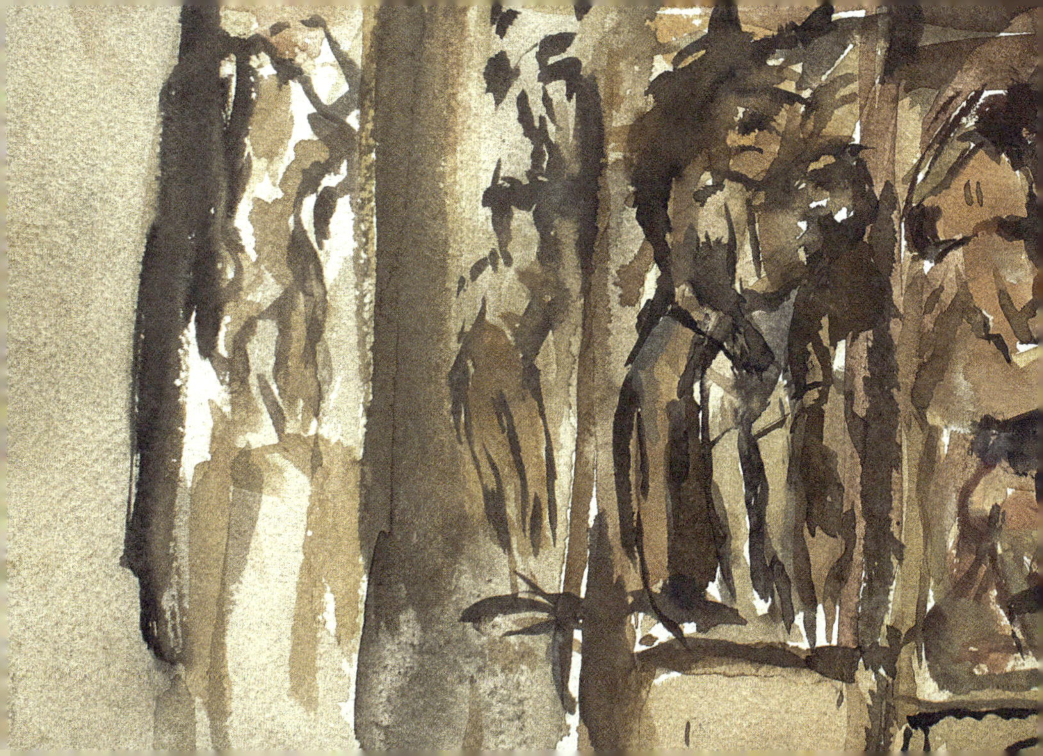

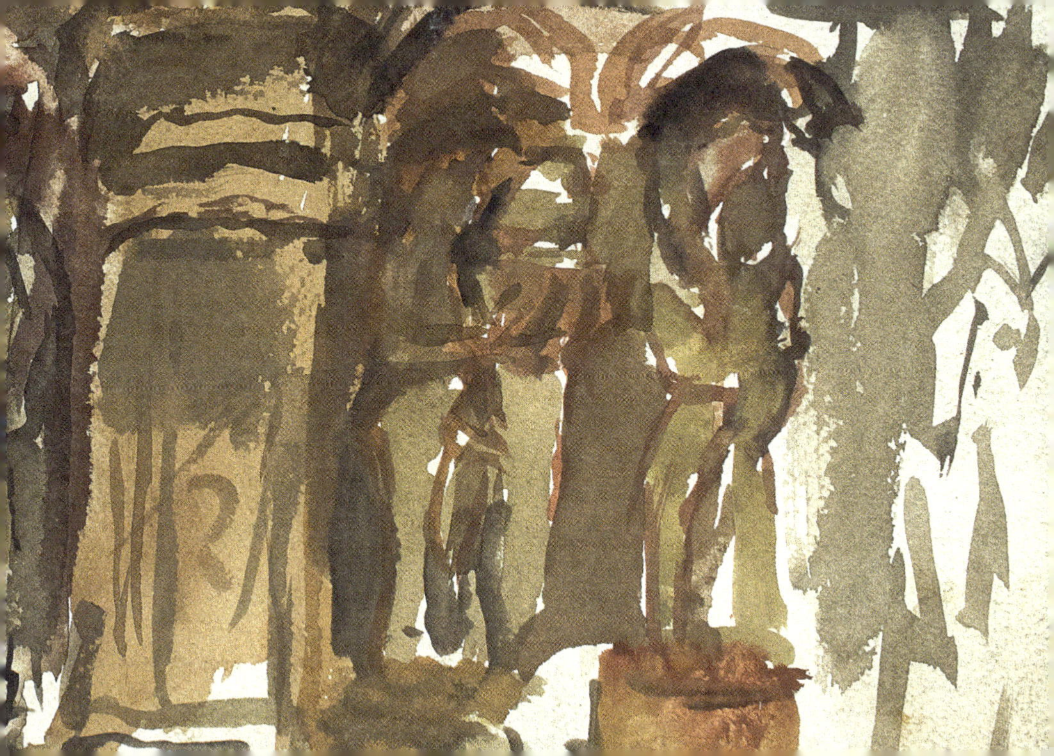

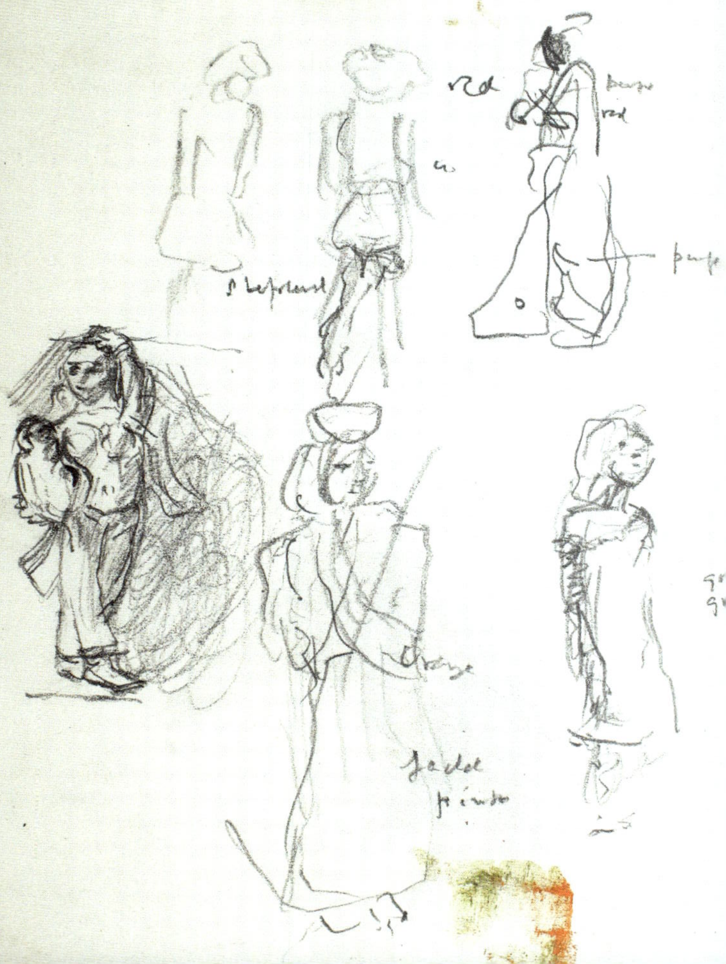
red
red
Shepherd
Orange

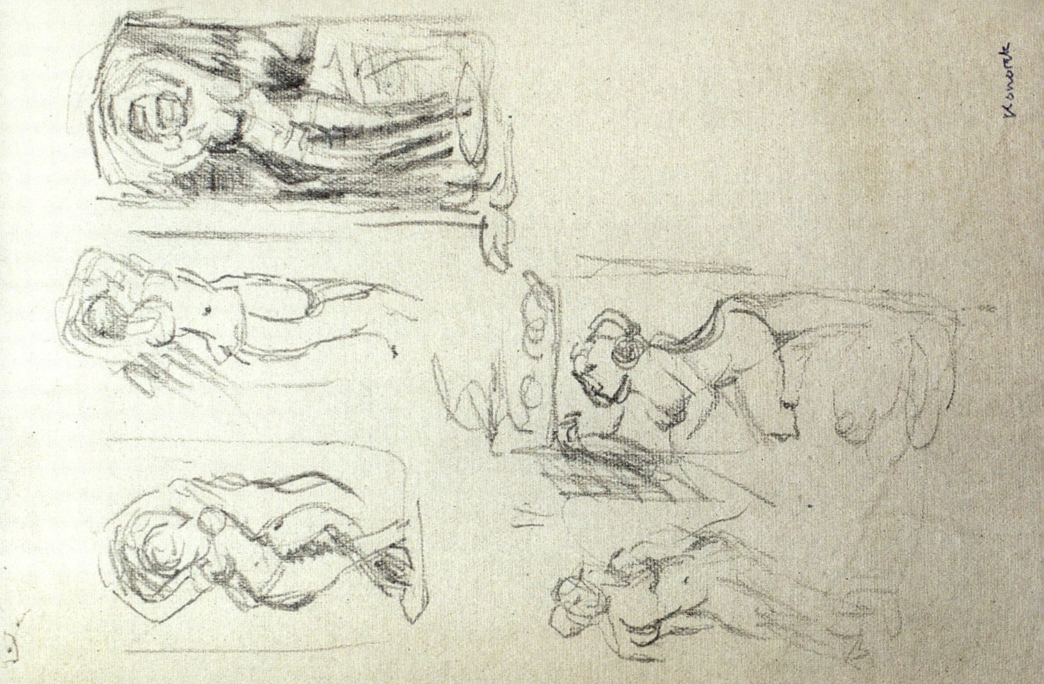

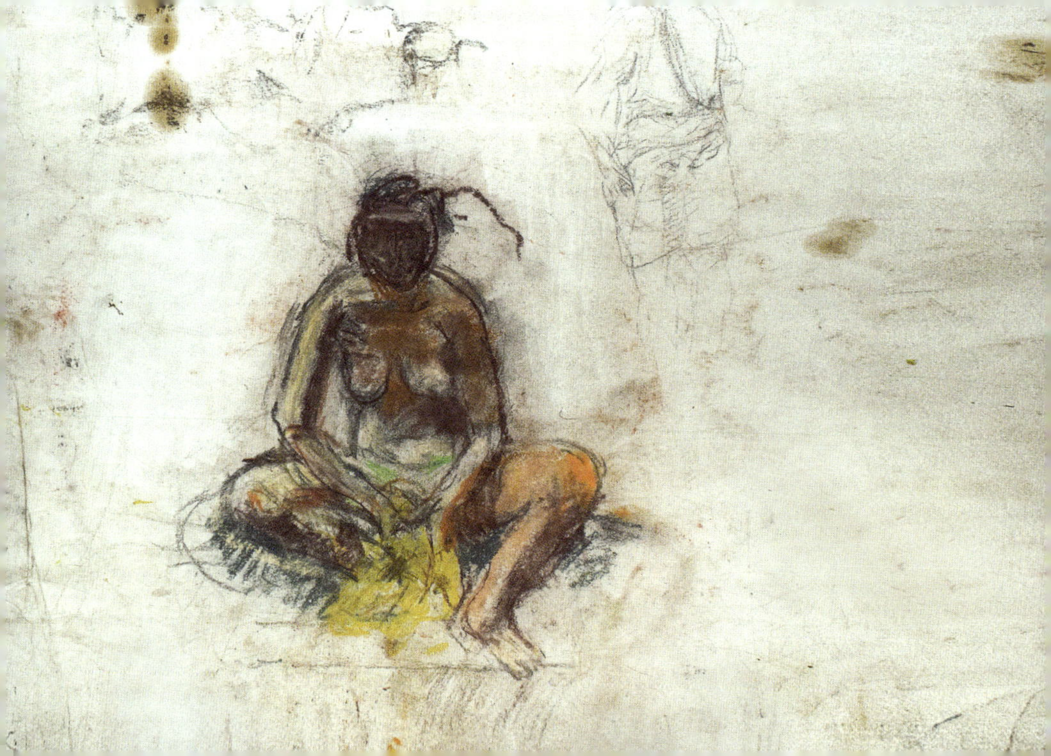

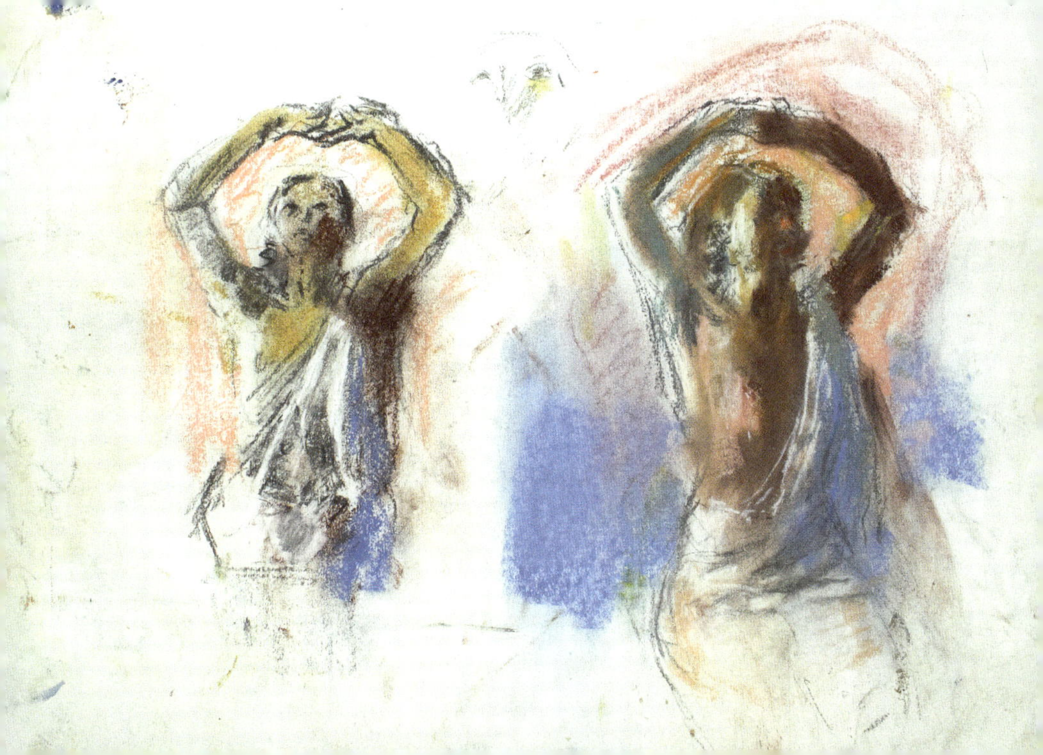

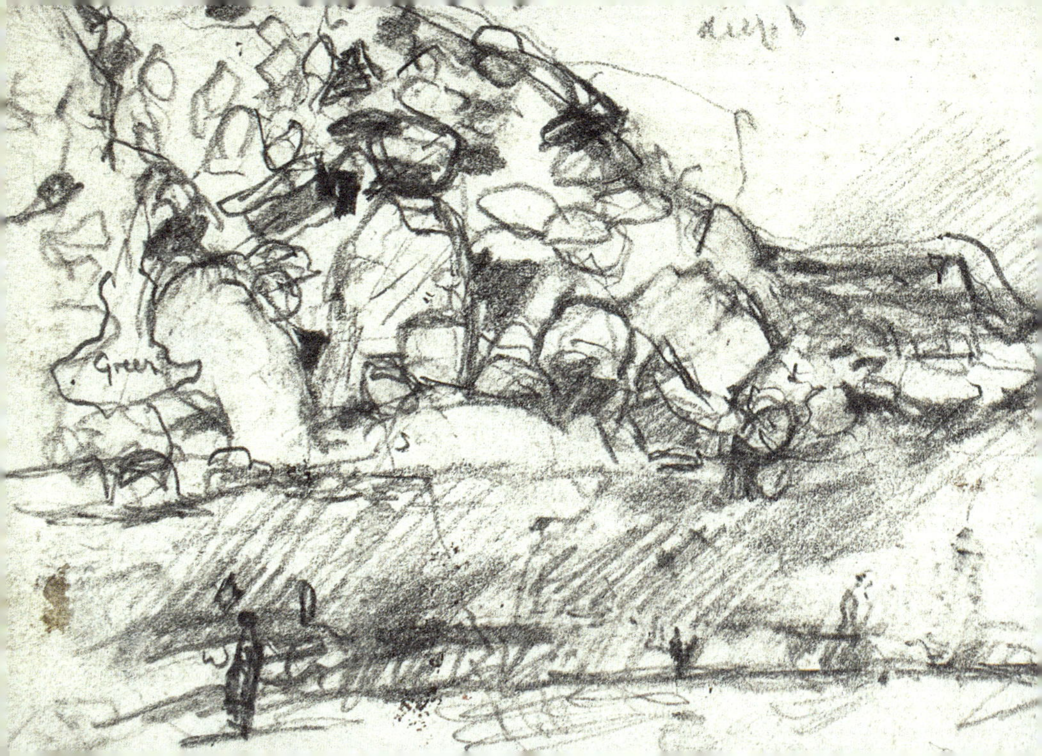
Green

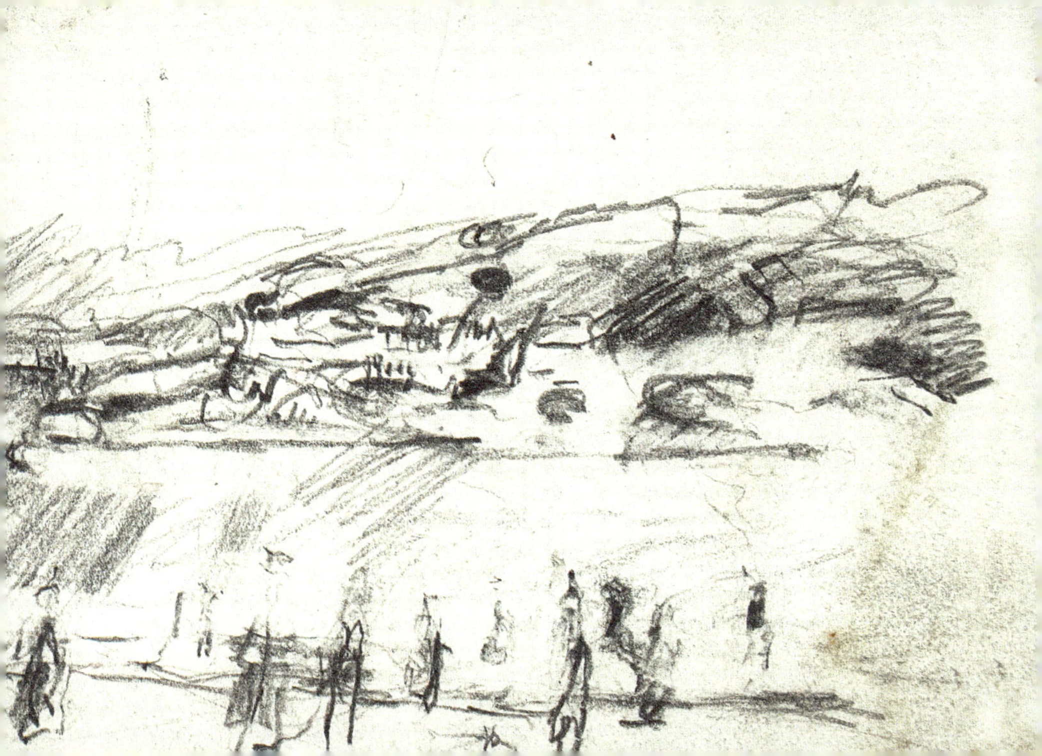

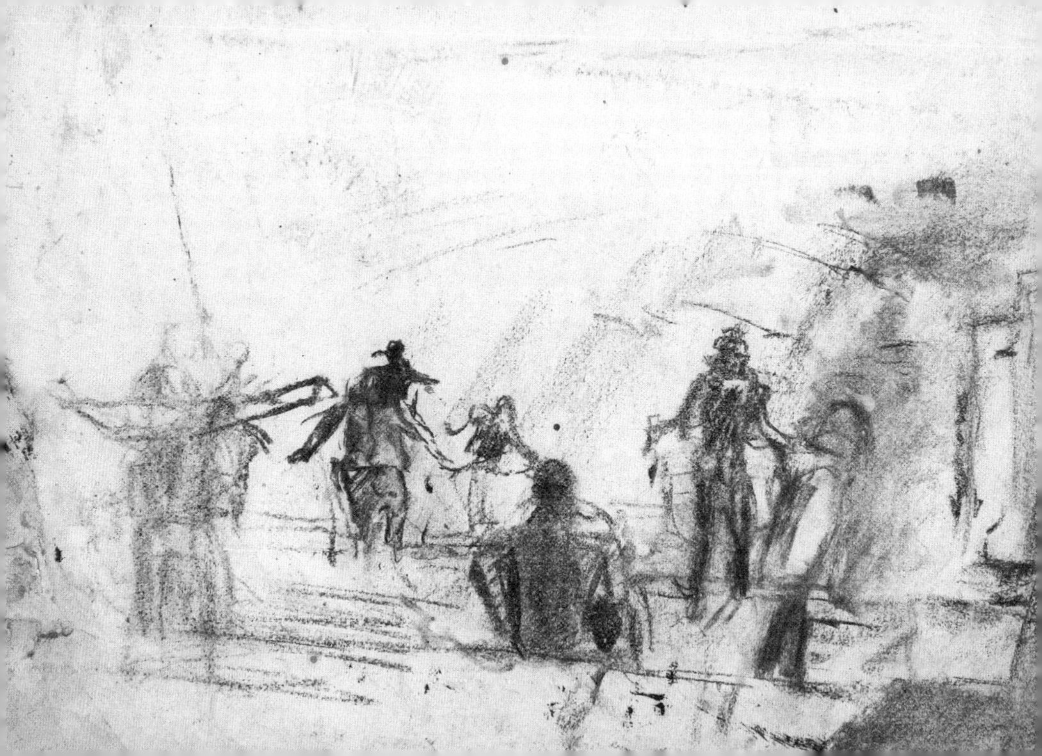

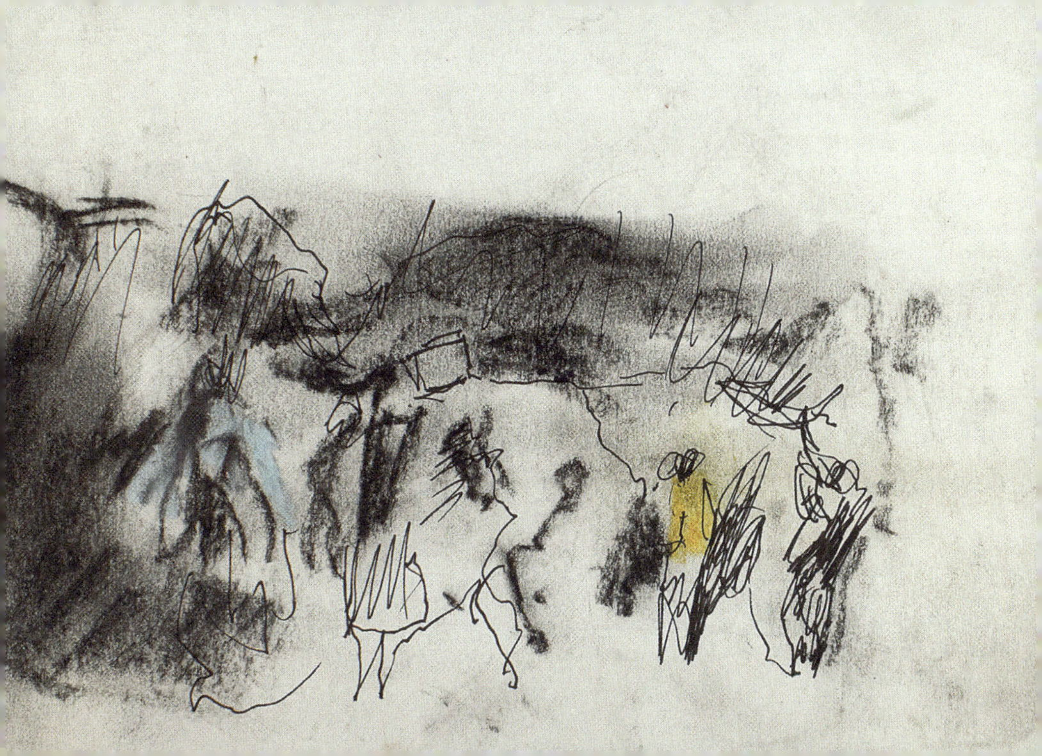

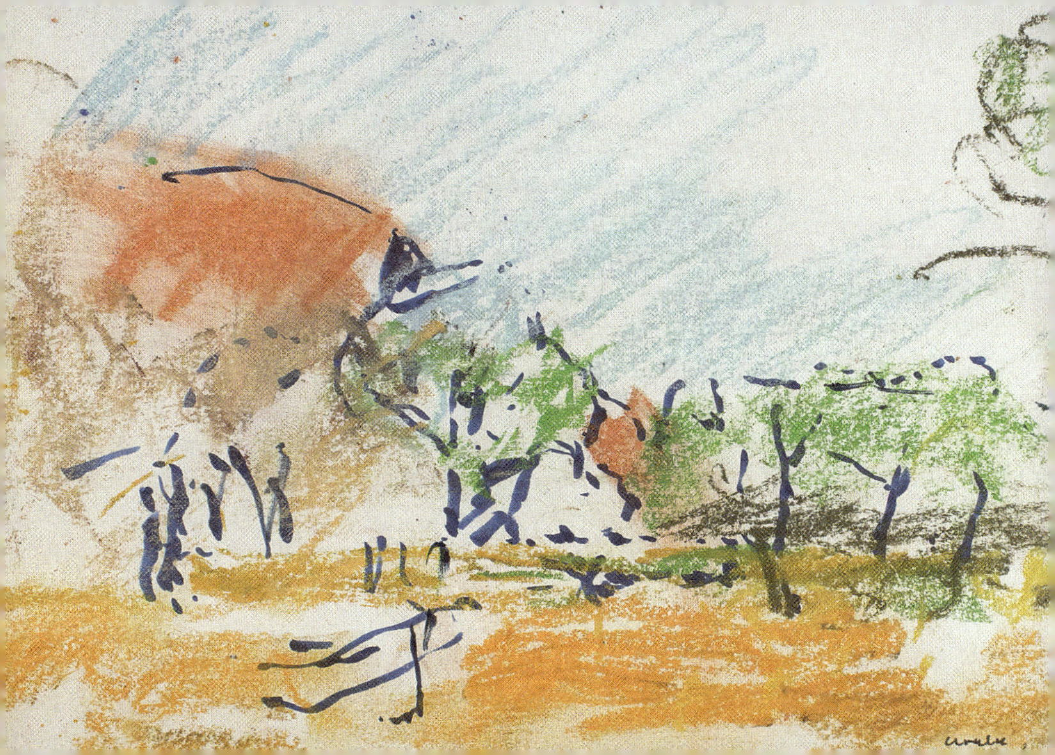

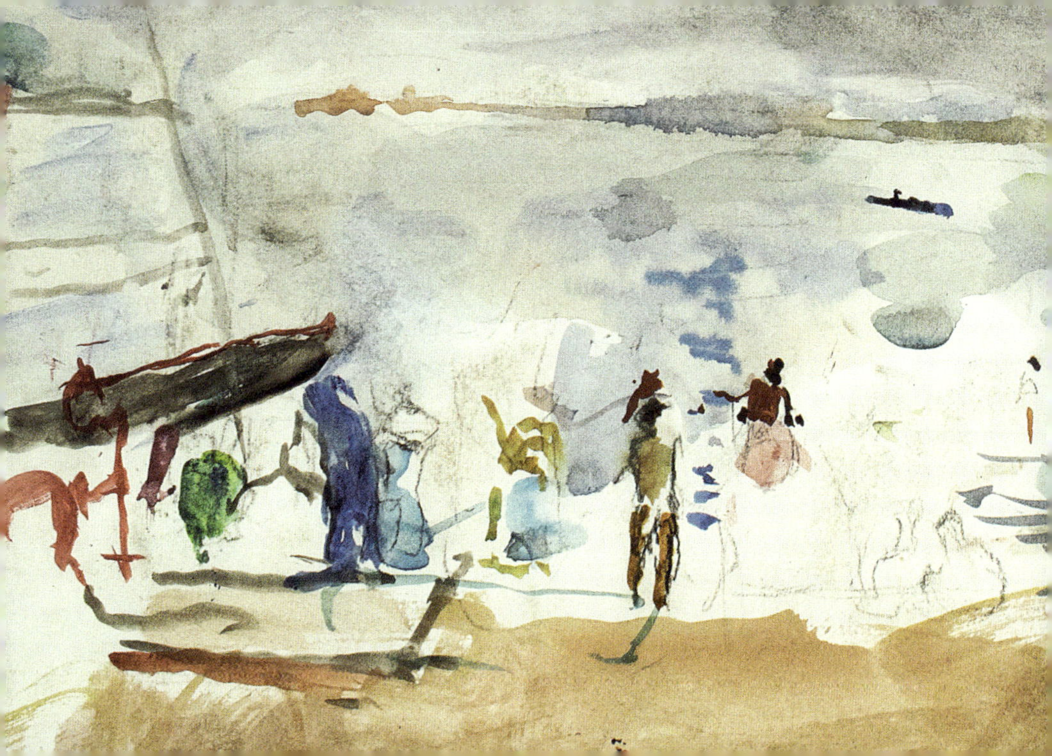

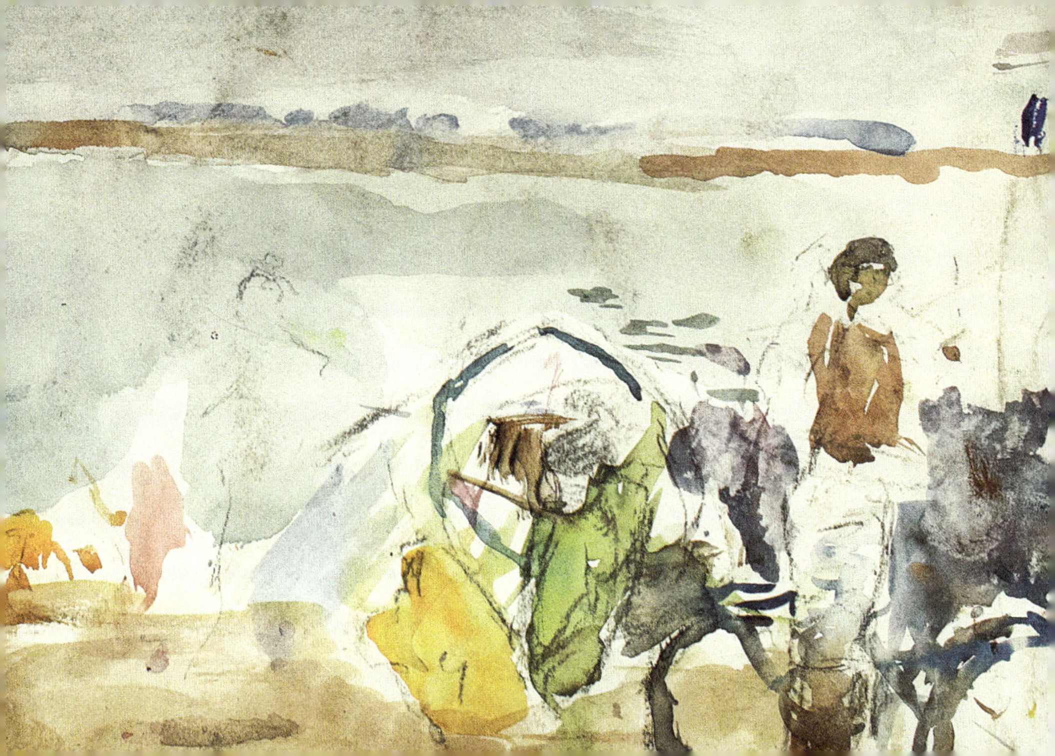

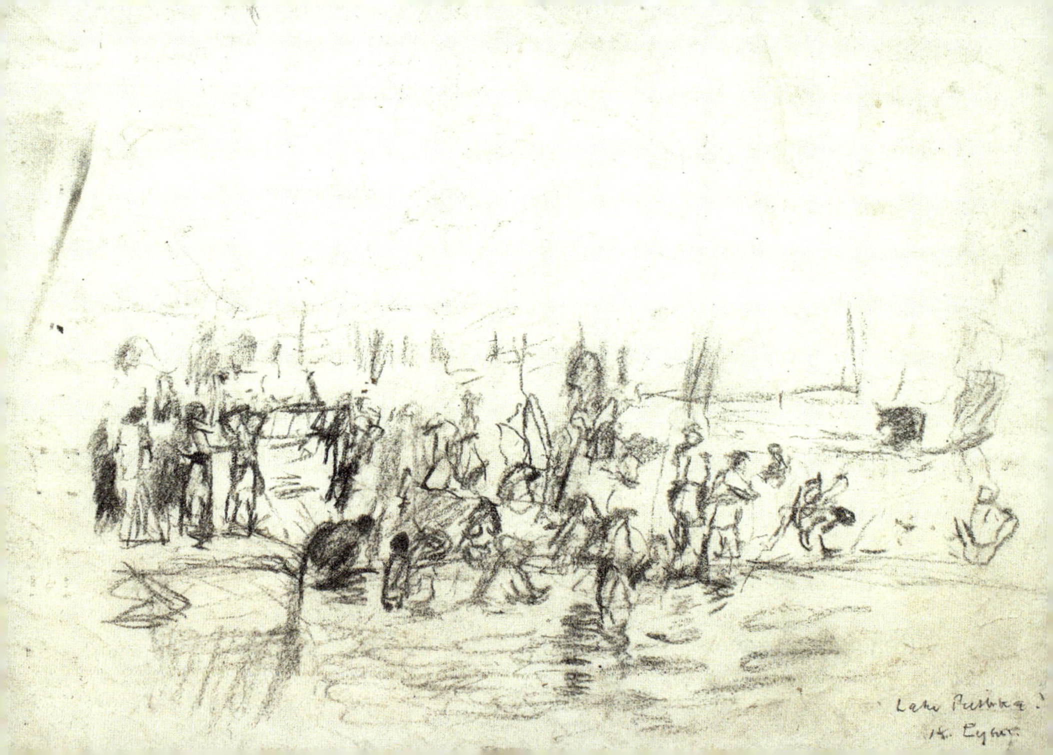
Lake Pushkar

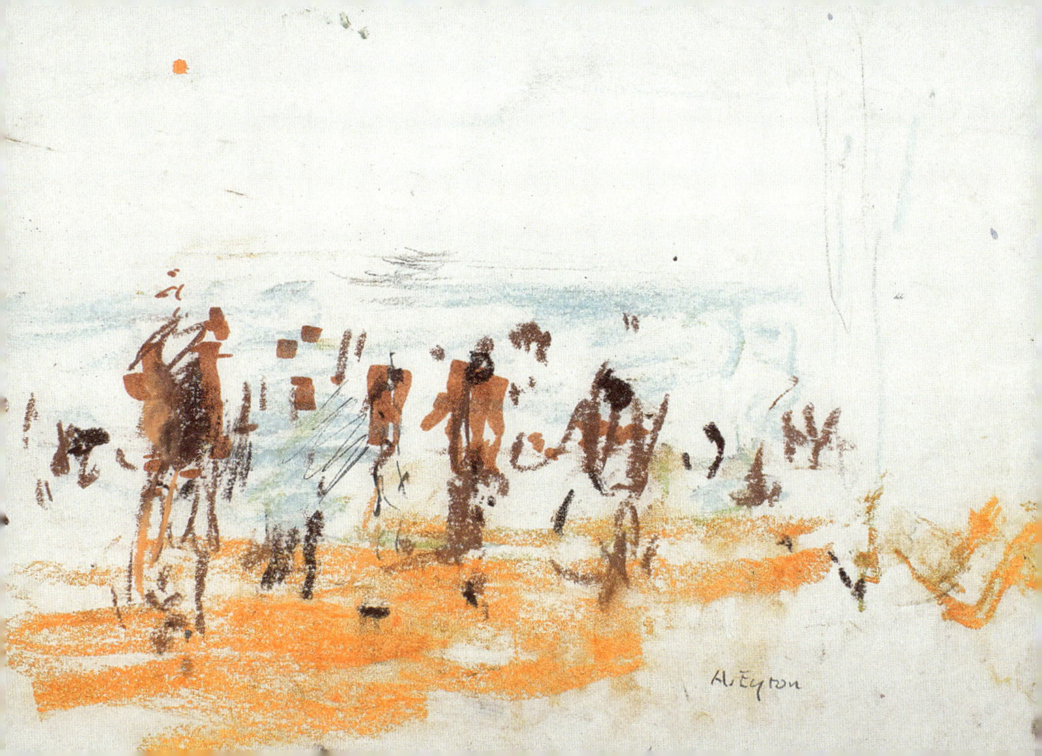
A. Eyton

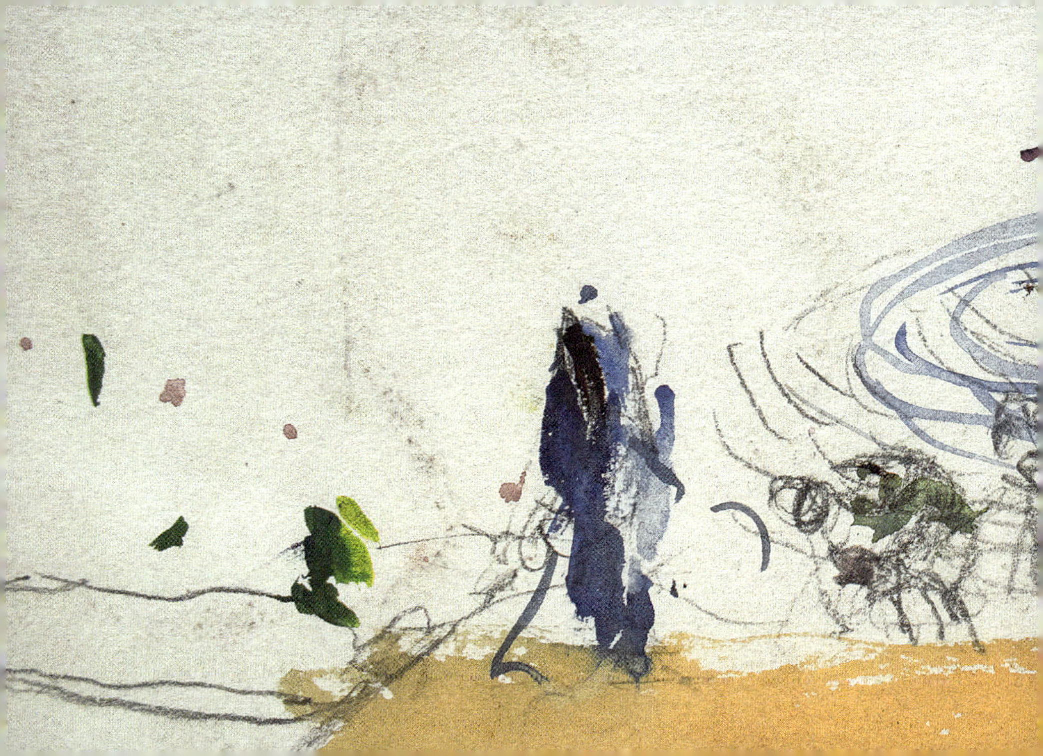

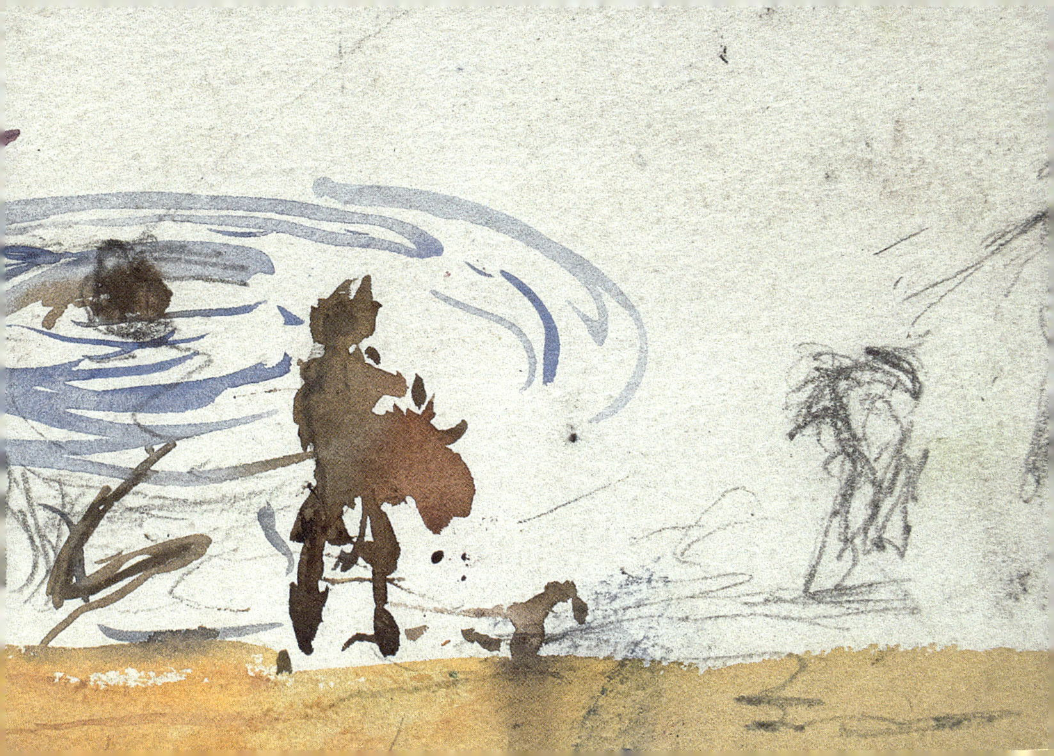

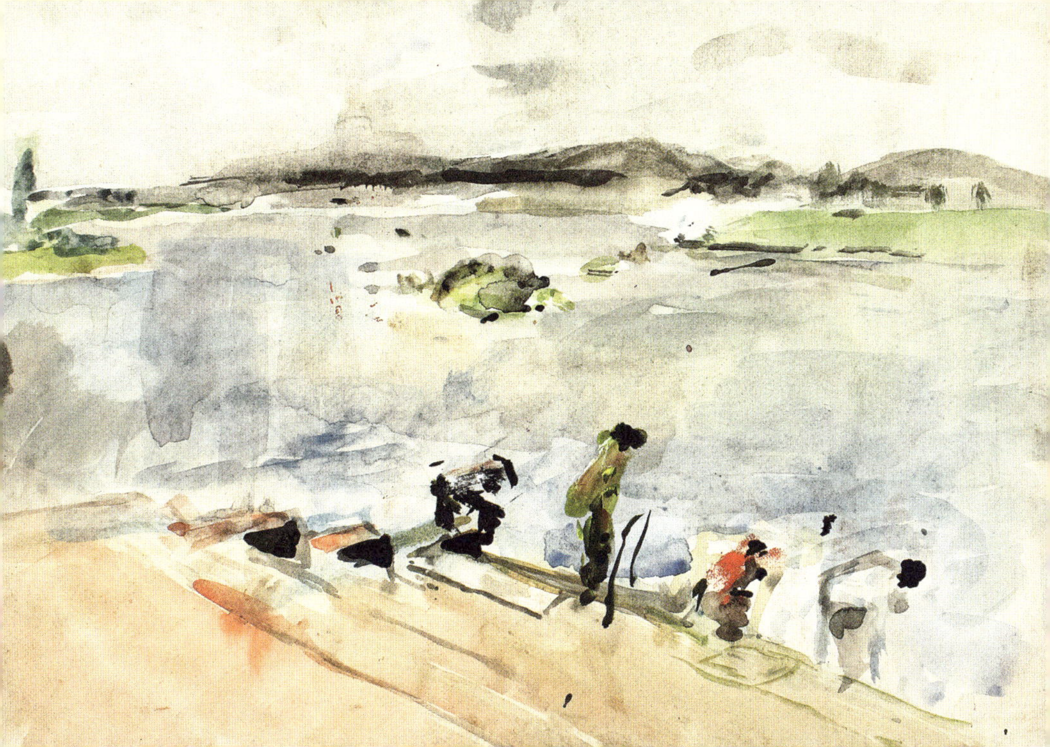

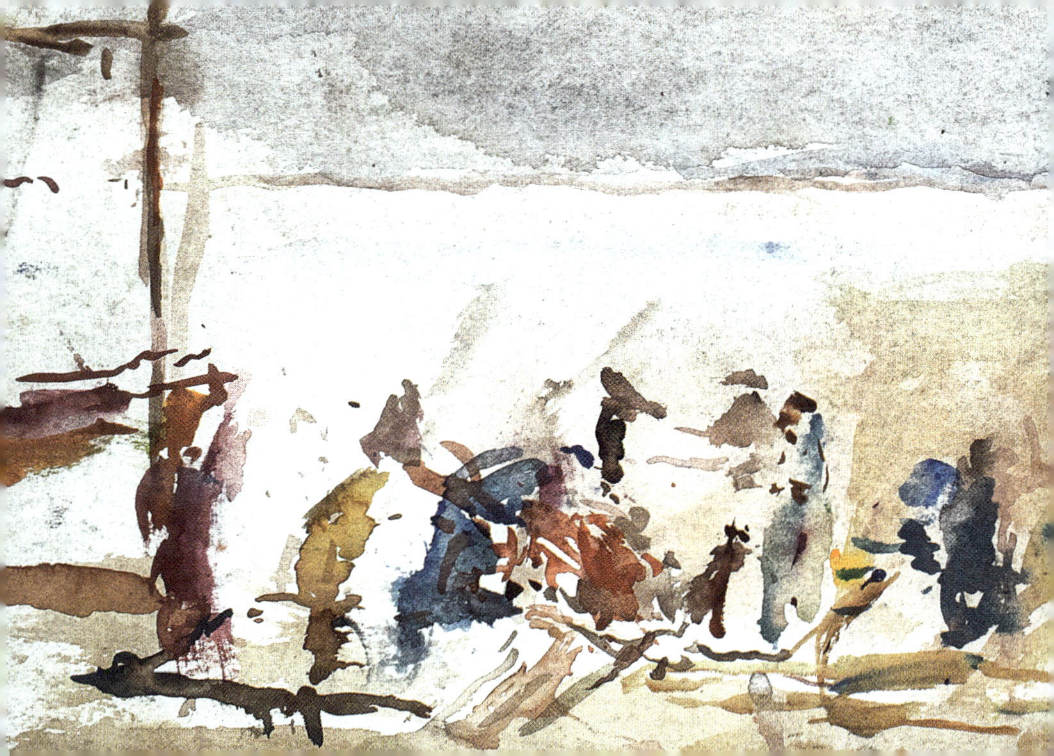

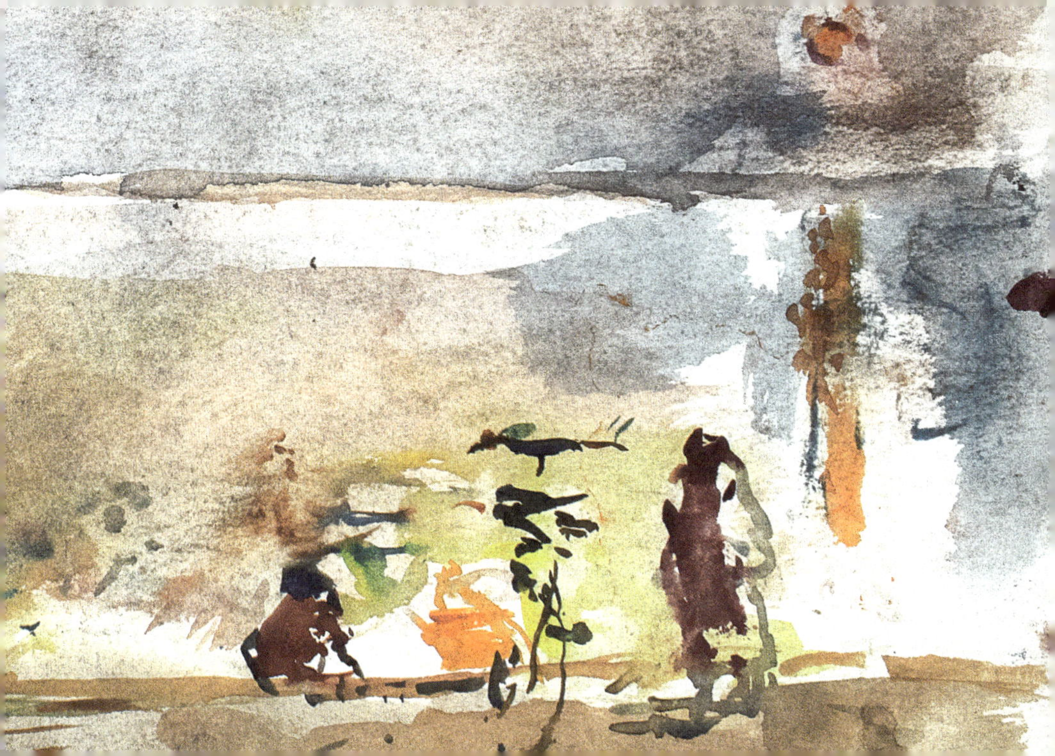

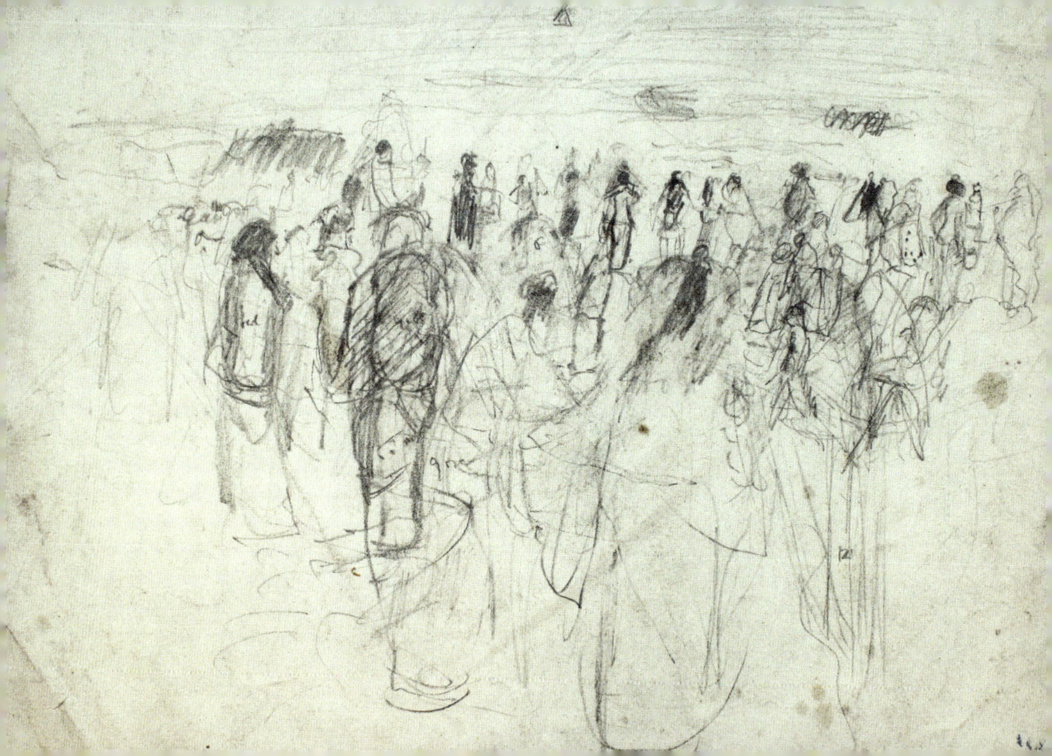

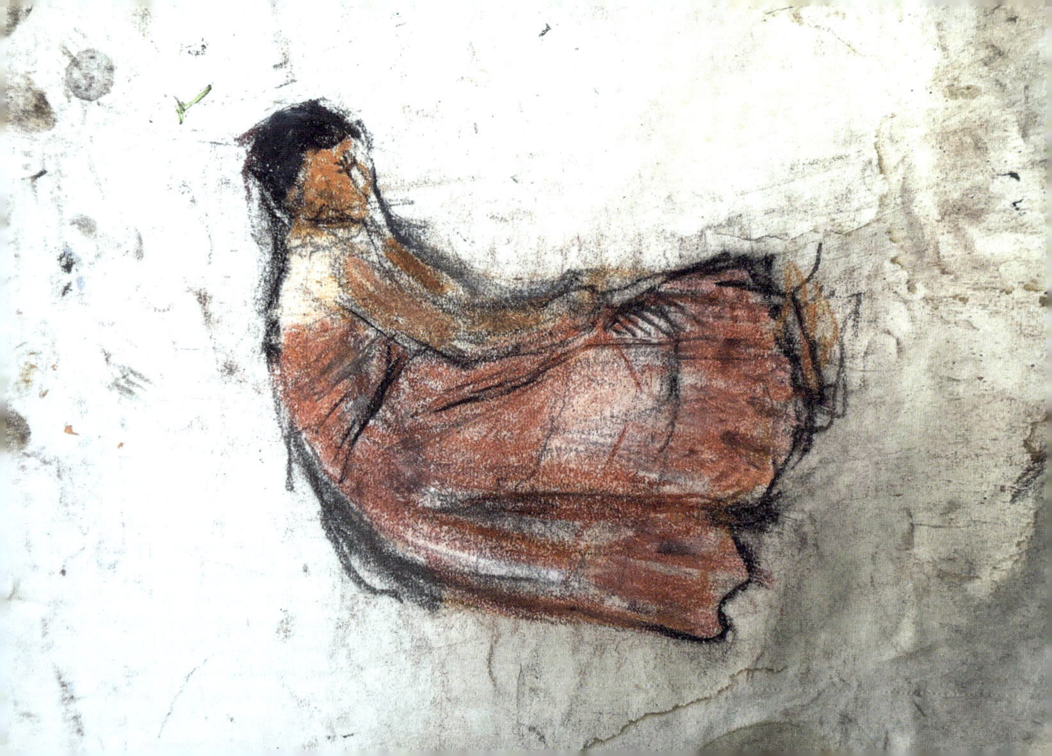

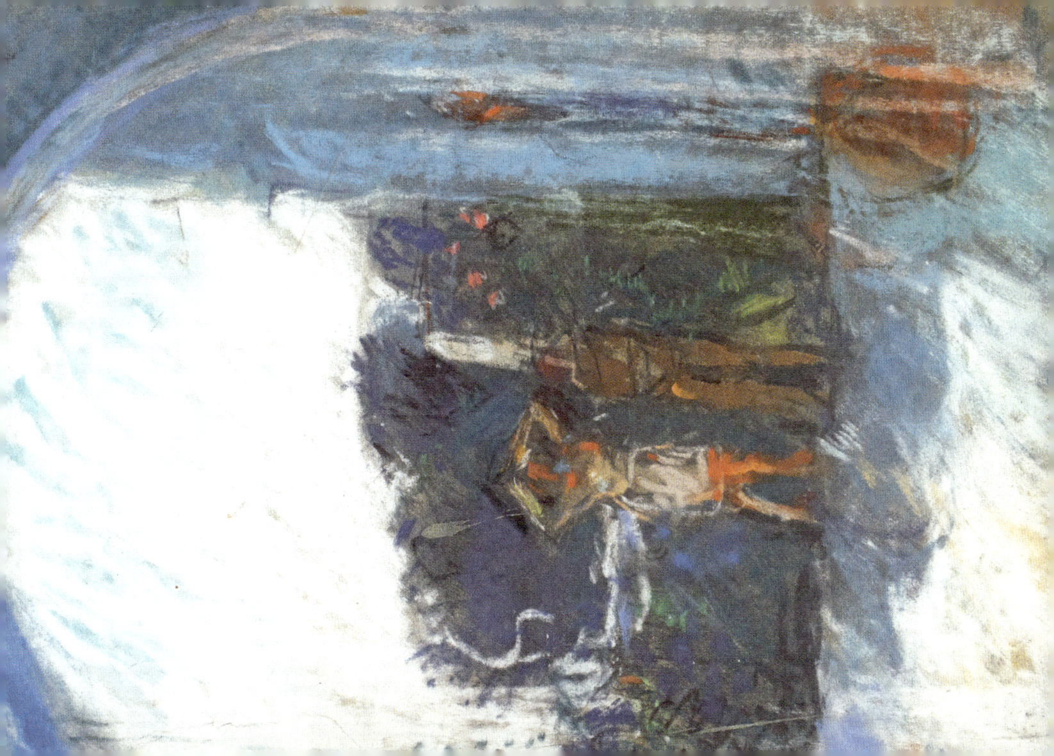

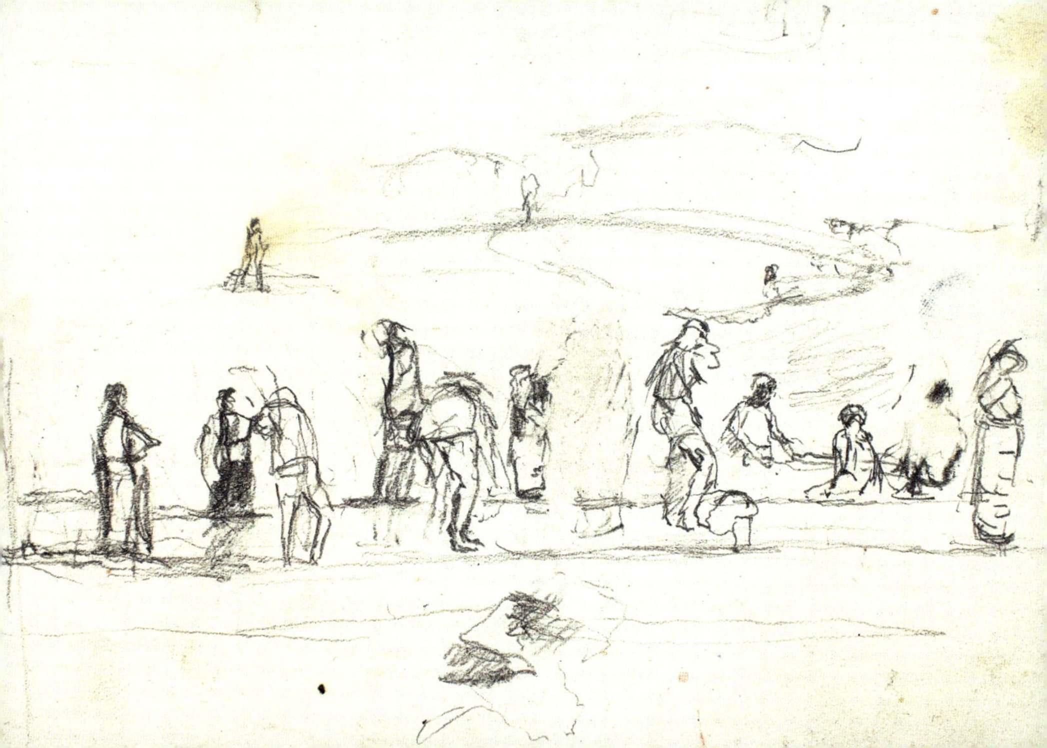

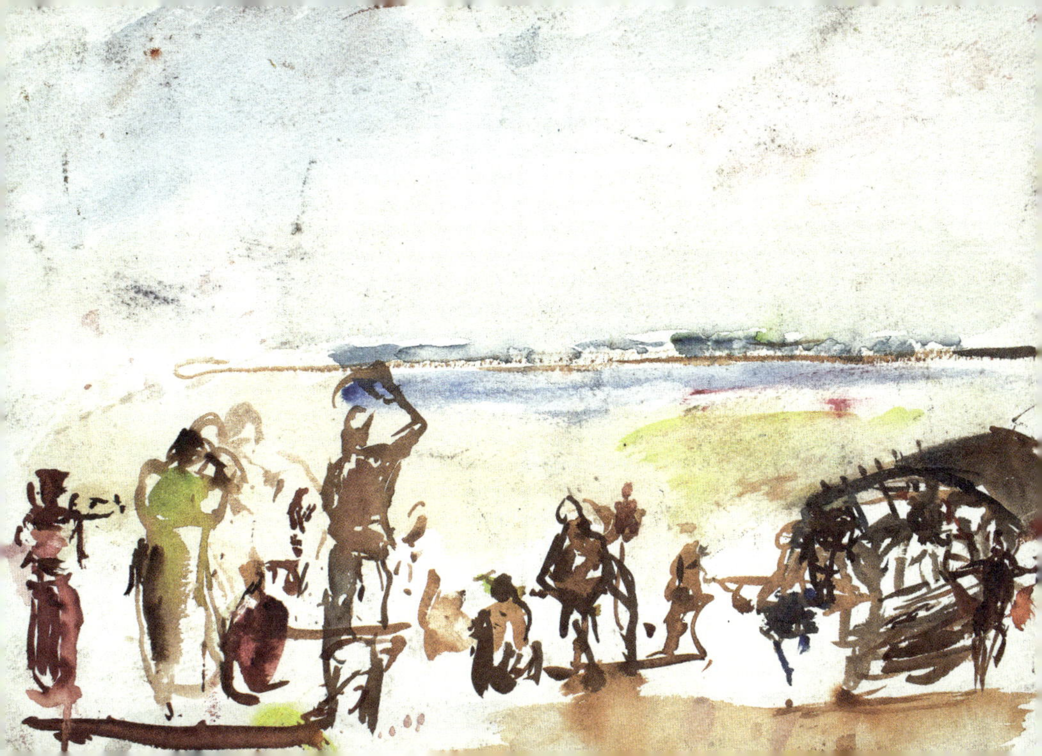

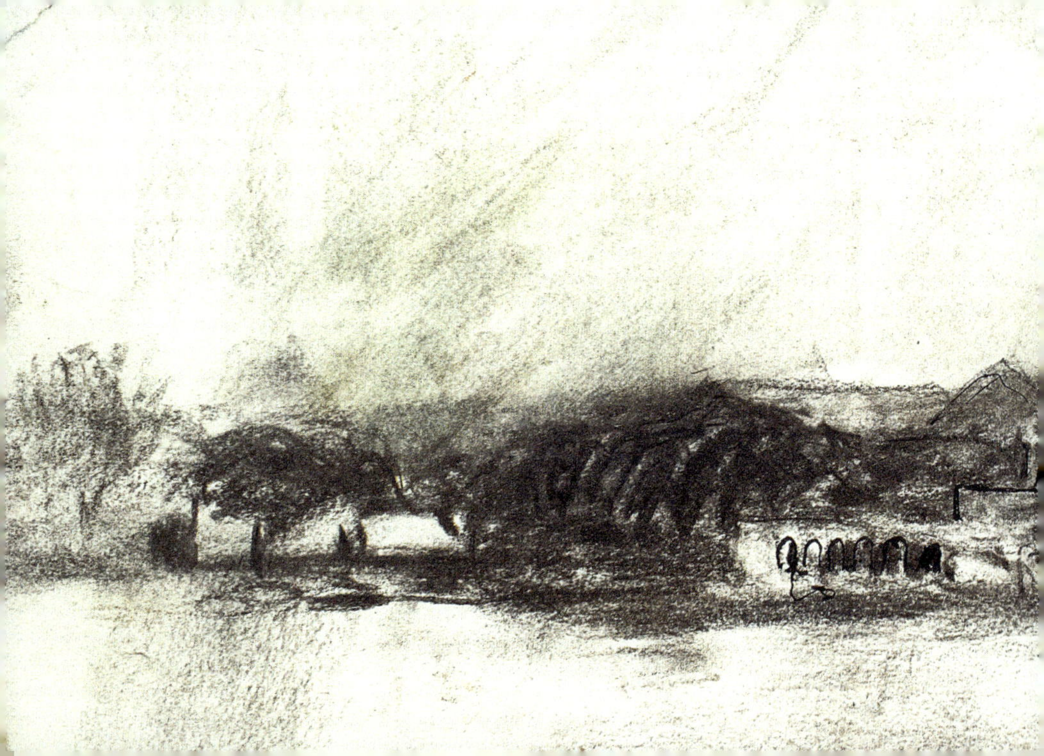

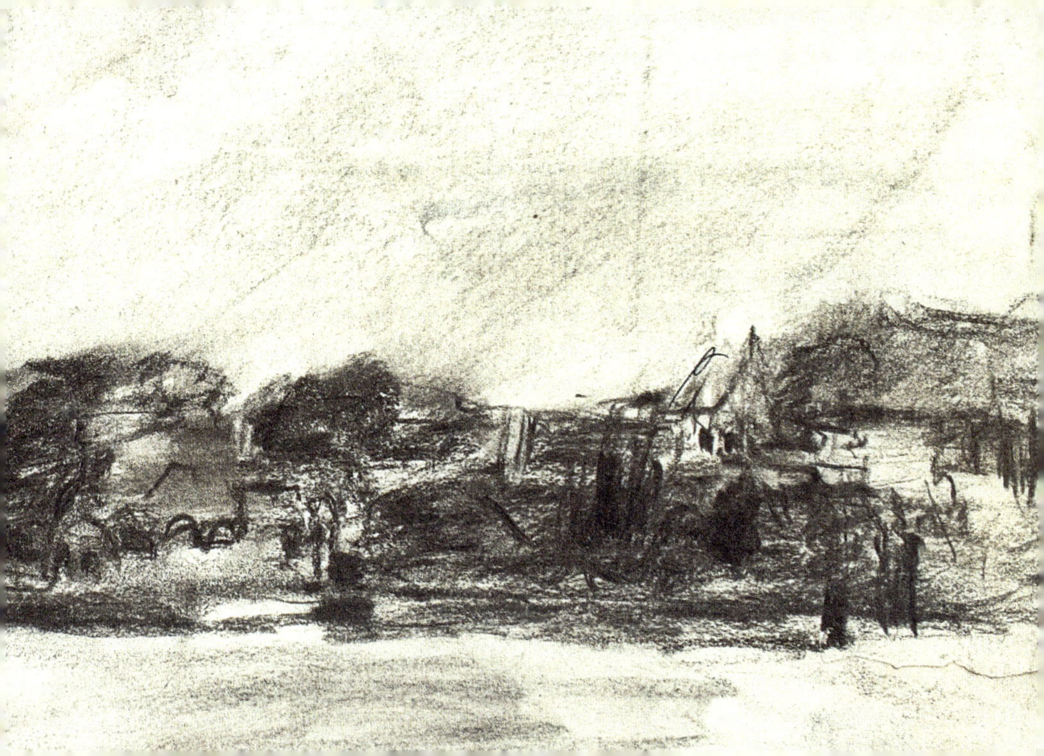

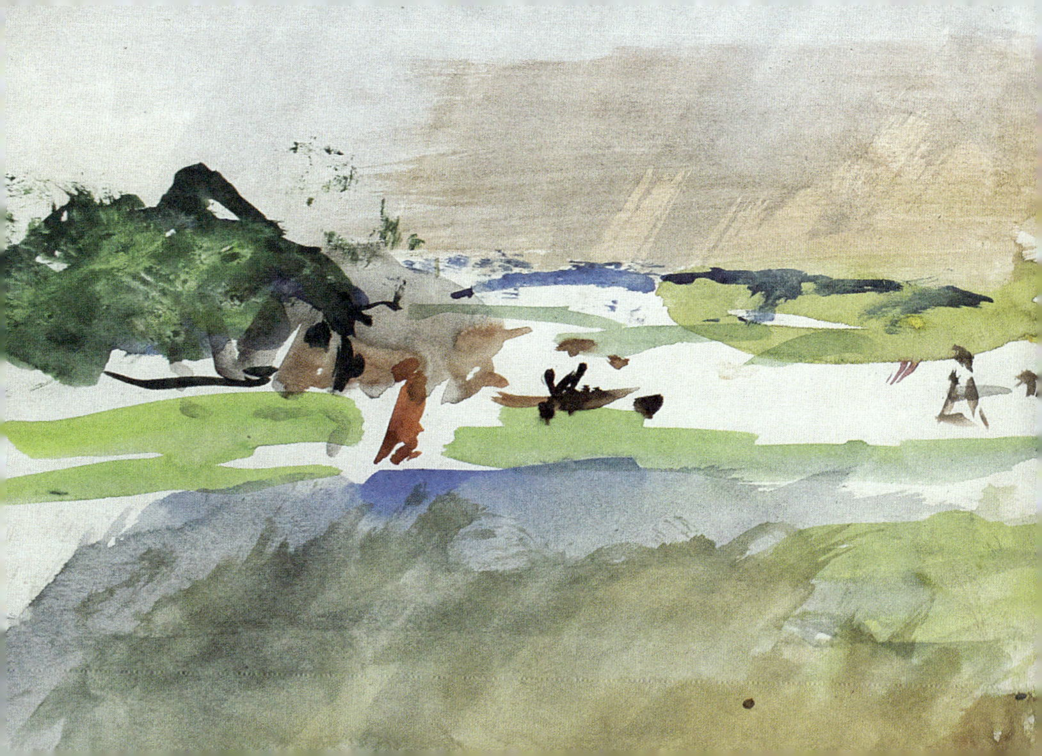

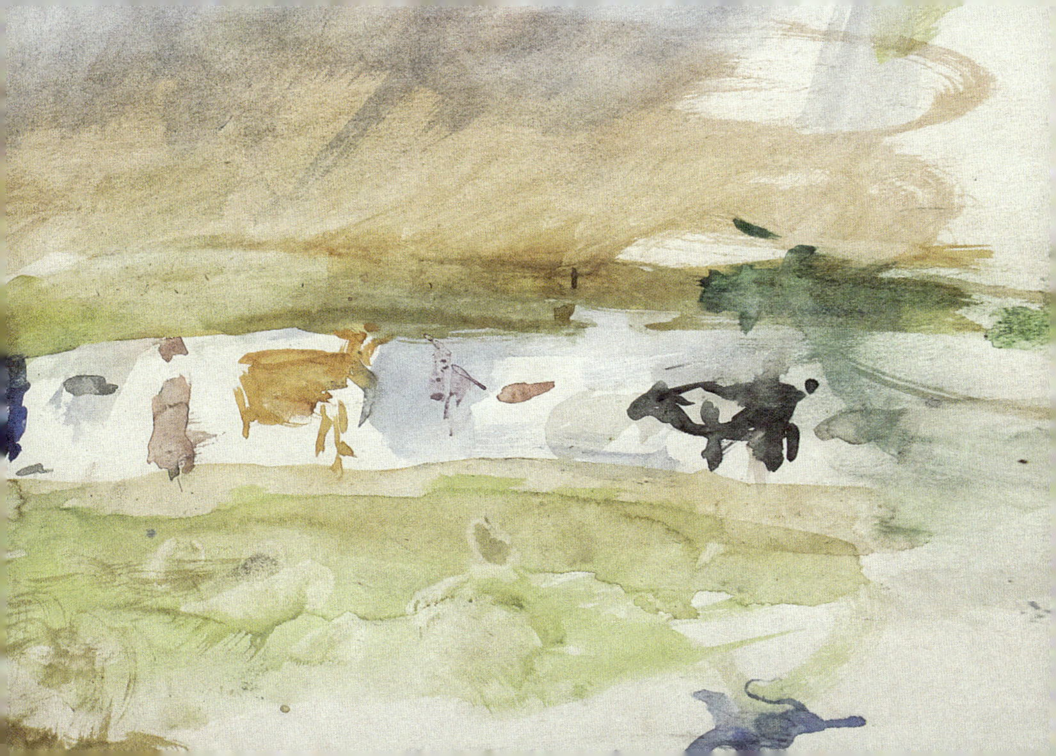

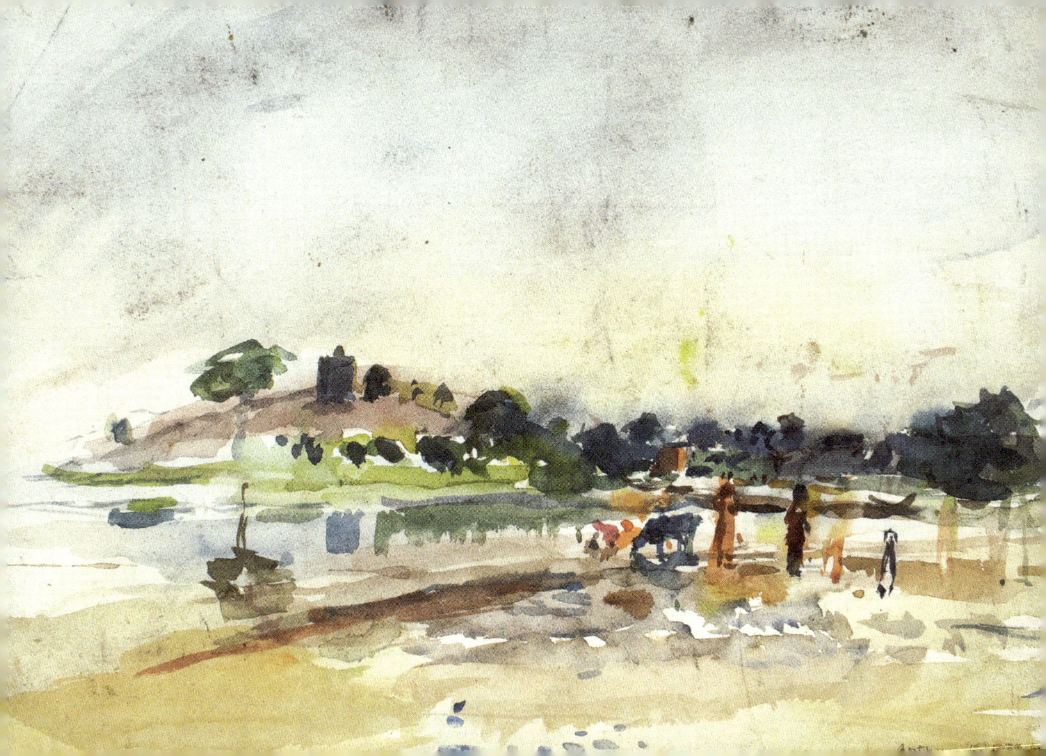

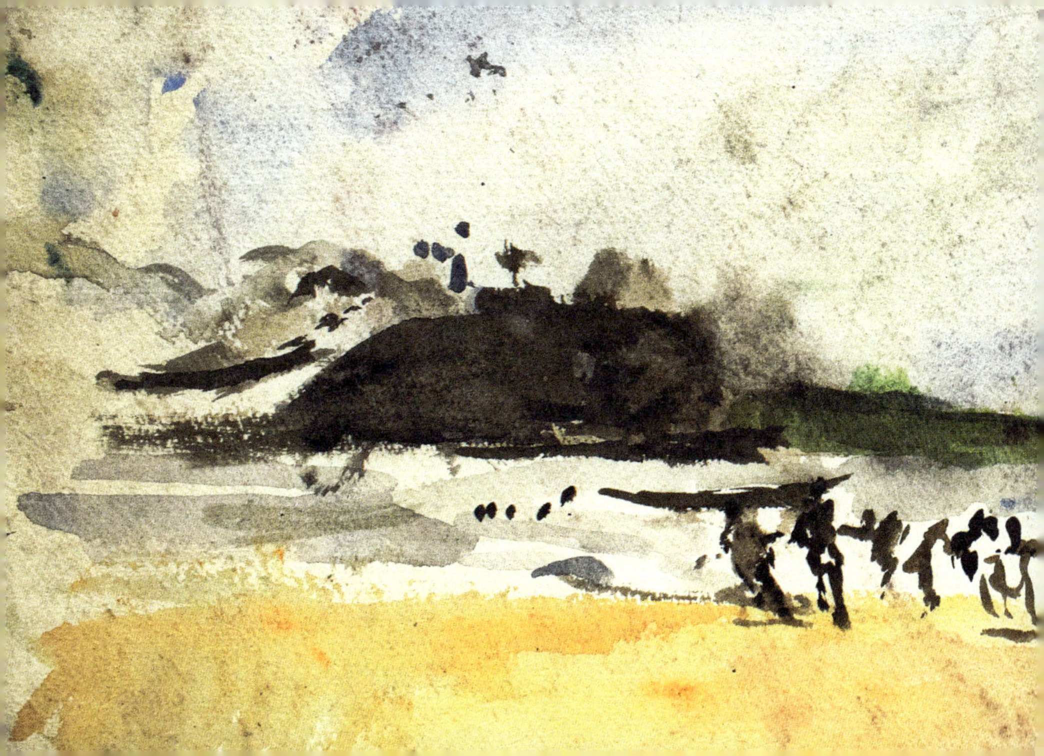

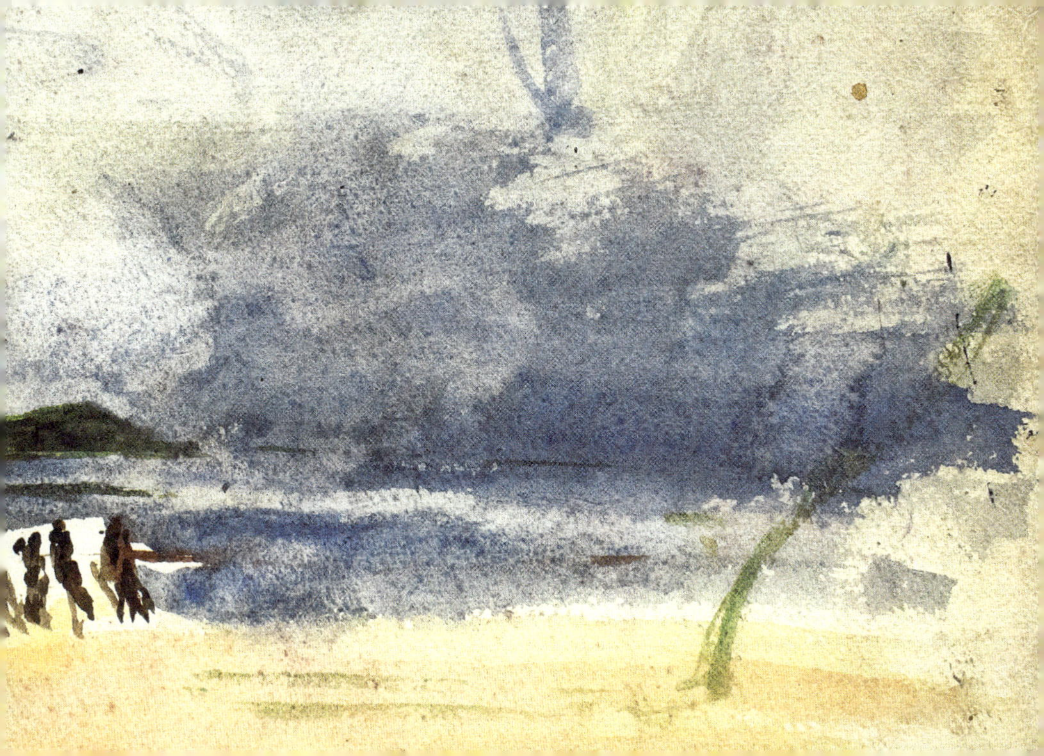

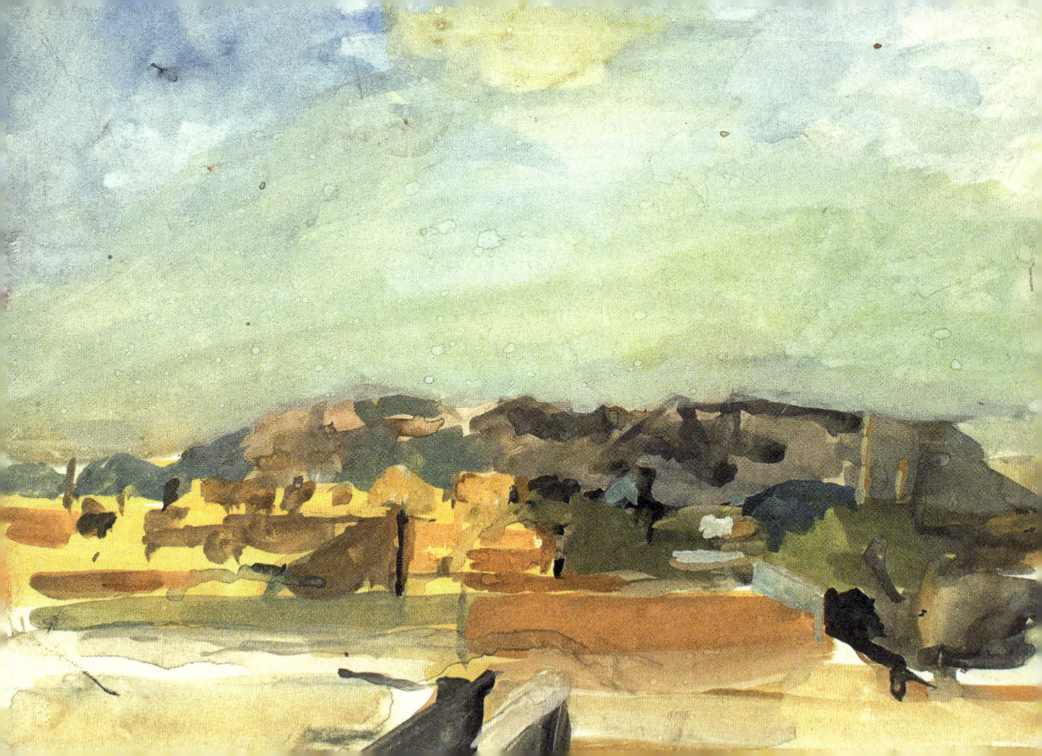

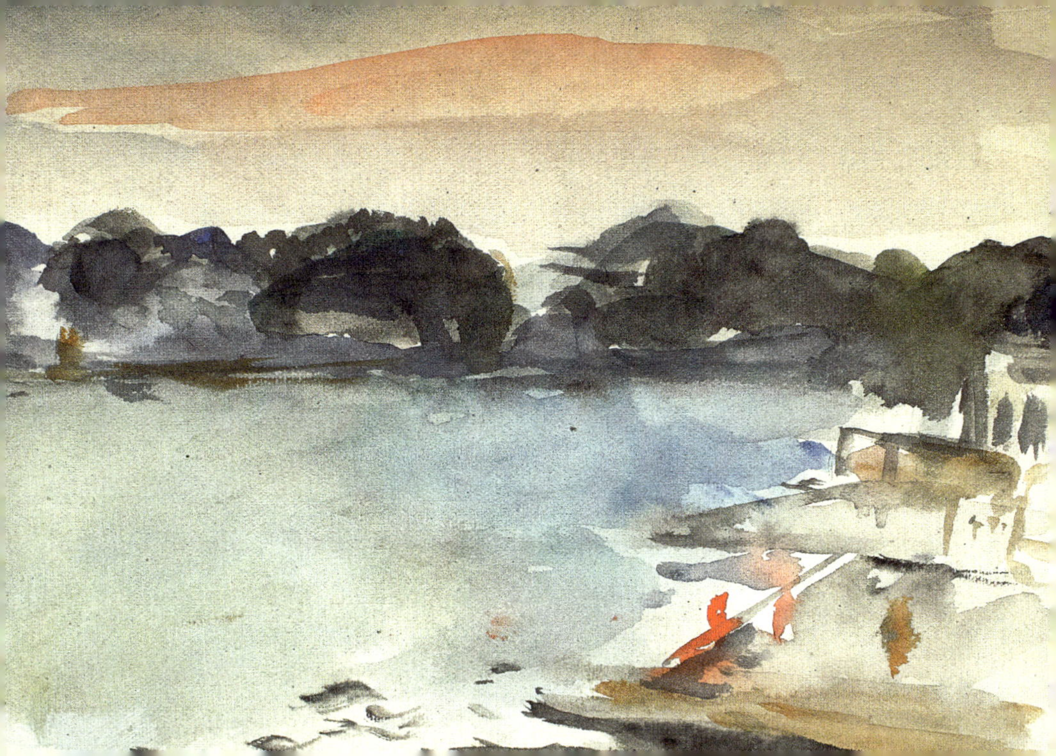

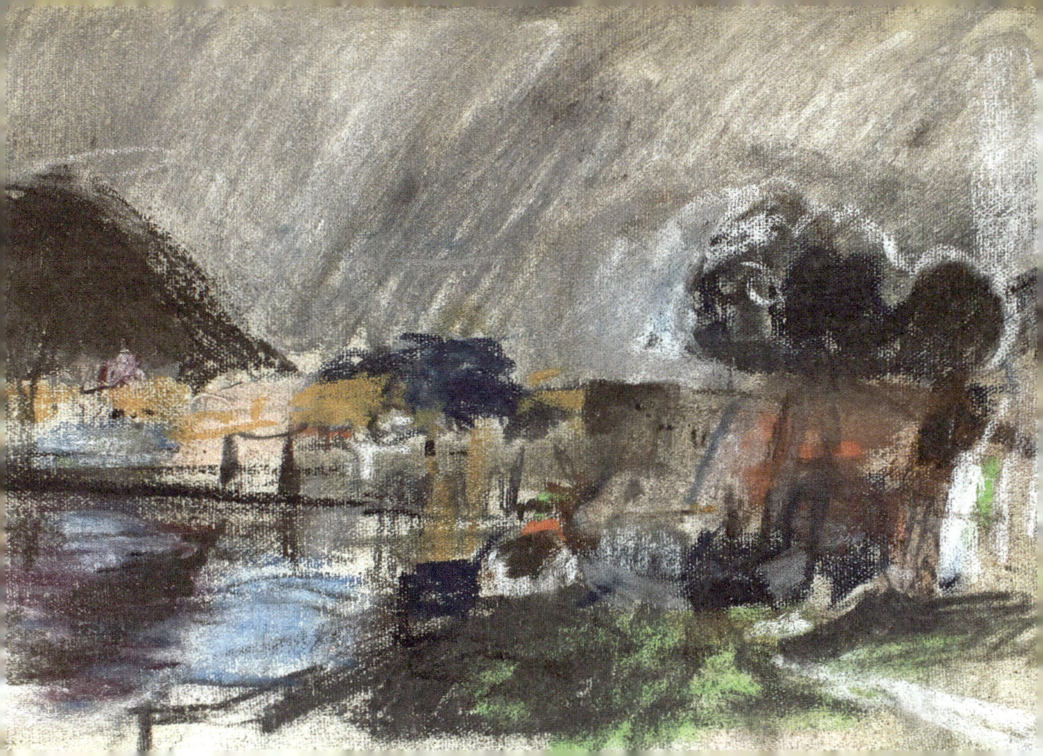

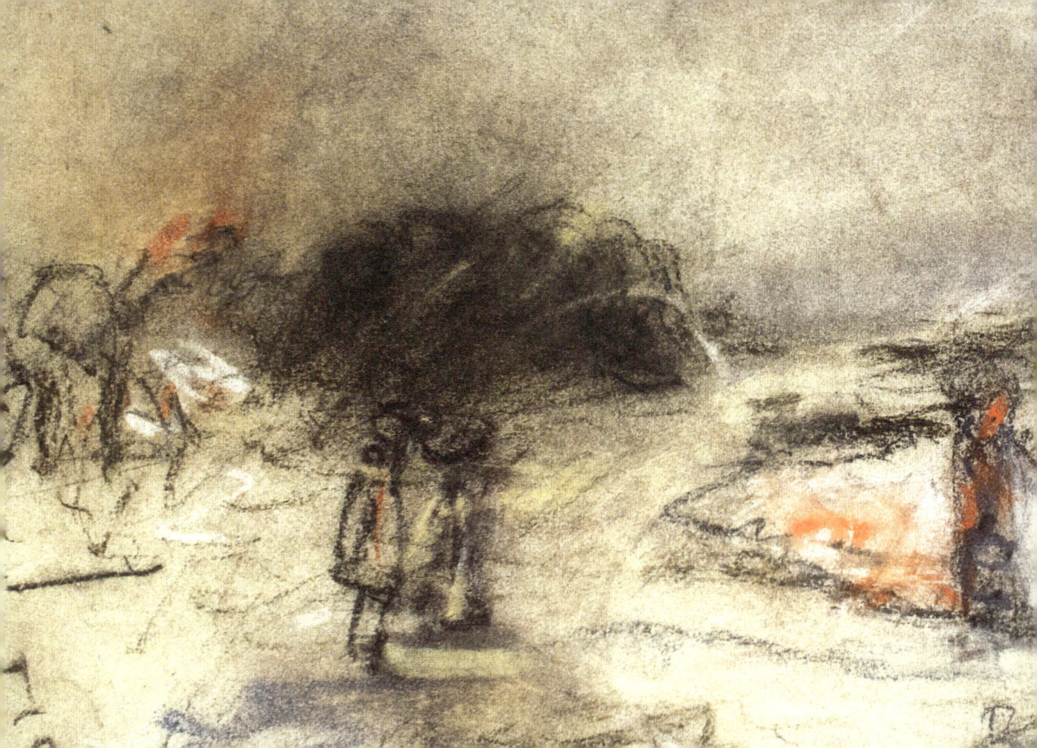

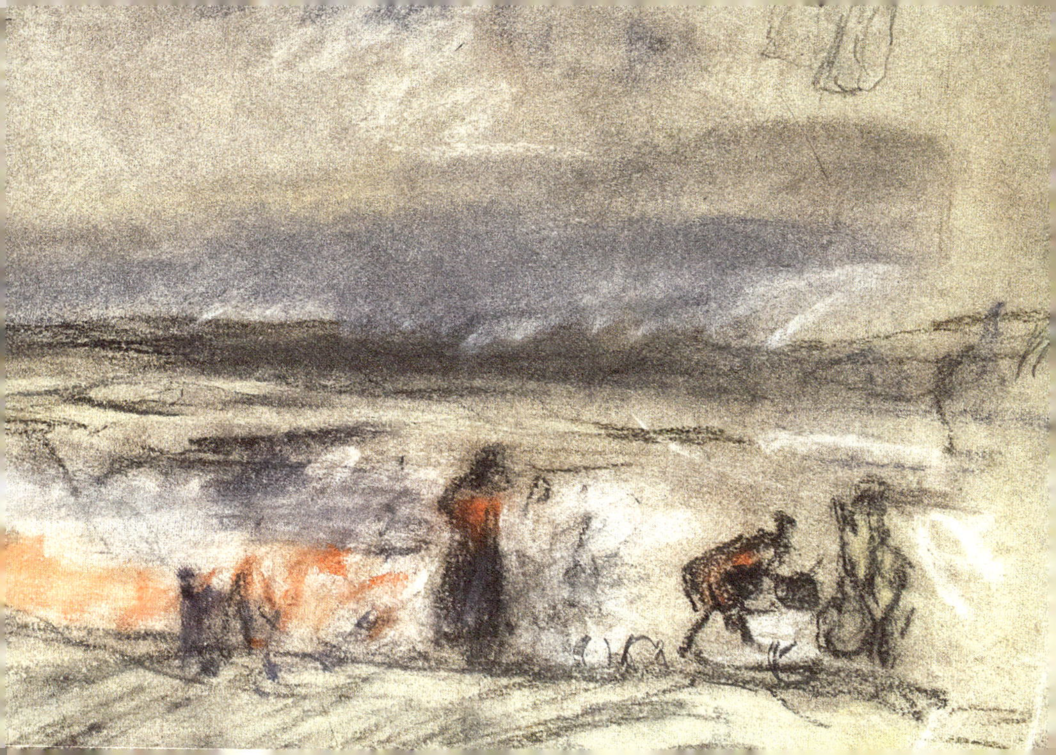

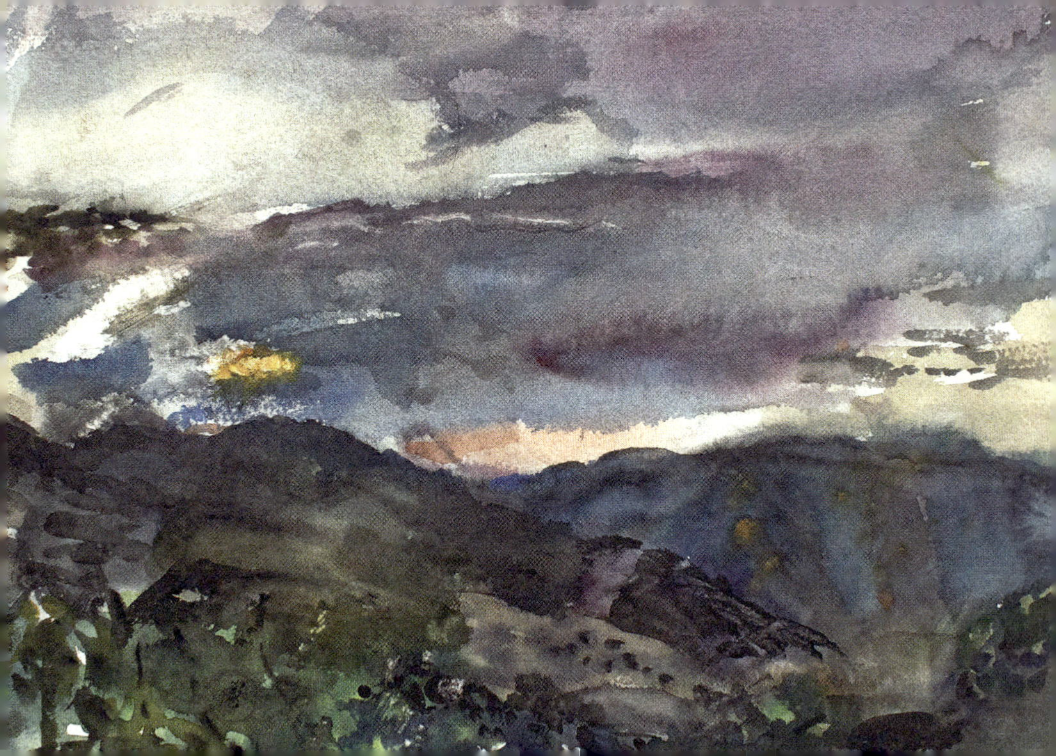

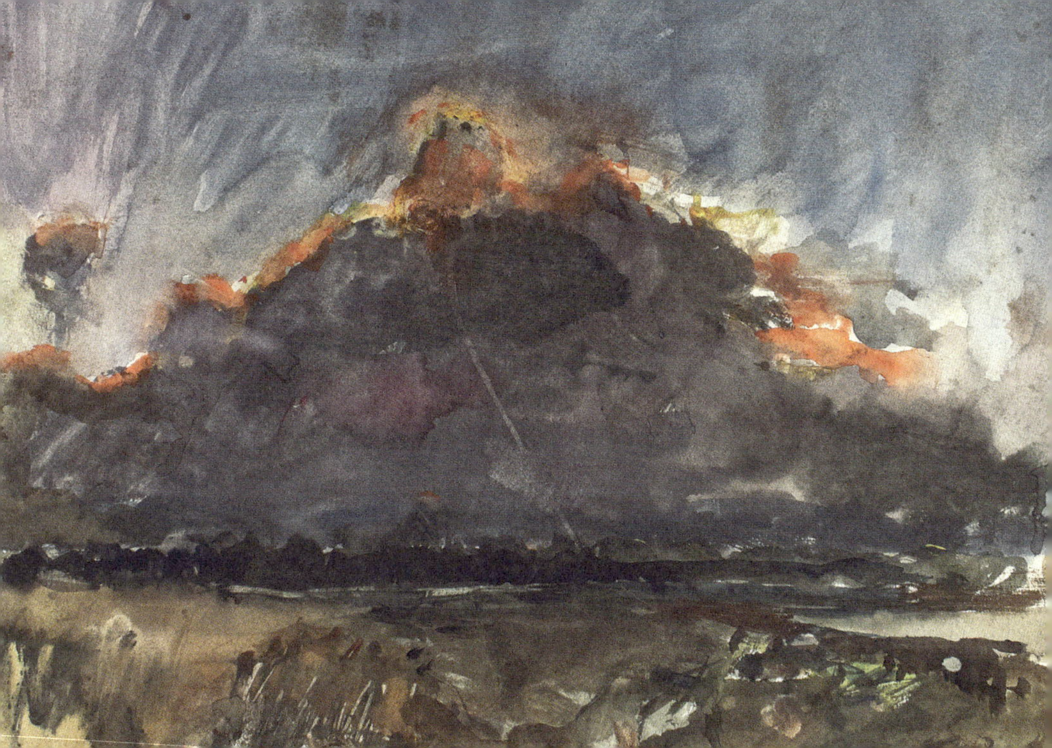

ROYAL ACADEMY PUBLICATIONS
Florence Dassonville, Production and Distribution Co-ordinator
Carola Krueger, Production and Distribution Manager
Peter Sawbridge, Head of Publishing and Editorial Director

Design: Maggi Smith
Printed in Italy by Lego, Vicenza

Royal Academy of Arts
Burlington House
Piccadilly
London W1J 0BD
www.royalacademy.org.uk

EU Authorised Representative
EAS Europe, Mustamäe tee 50, 10621 Tallinn, Estonia. gpsr.requests@easproject.com

British Library Cataloguing-in-Publication Data
A catalogue record for this book is available from the British Library

ISBN 978-1-915815-21-7

Distributed outside the United States and Canada by ACC Art Books Ltd, Riverside House, Dock Lane, Melton, Woodbridge, IP12 1PE

Distributed in the United States and Canada by ACC Art Books, 6 West 18th Street, Suite 4B, New York, NY 10011